W9-ADM-019

The Question of Zion

The Question of Zion

Jacqueline Rose

PRINCETON UNIVERSITY PRESS

PRINCETON AND OXFORD

Requests for permission to reproduce material from this work should be sent to Permissions, Princeton University Press
Published by Princeton University Press, 41 William Street, Princeton, New Jersey 08540
In the United Kingdom: Princeton University Press, 3 Market Place, Woodstock, Oxfordshire OX20 1SY

Library of Congress Cataloging-in-Publication Data

Rose, Jacqueline.
The question of Zion / Jacqueline Rose.
p. cm.
Includes bibliographical references and index.
ISBN 0-691-11750-0 (alk. paper)
1. Zionism—History—20th century. 2. Zionism—Psychological aspects. 3. Arab-Israeli conflict—Psychological aspects. 4. Palestinian Arabs—Crimes against—Israel. 5. Psychoanalysis—Political aspects—Israel. 6. Holocaust, Jewish (1939–1945)—Influence. 7. Israel—Ethnic relations. I. Title.
DS149.R58 2005
320.54′095694—dc22 2004059993

British Library Cataloging-in-Publication Data is available

This book has been composed in Sabon with Insignia Display

Printed on acid-free paper. ∞

pup.princeton.edu

Printed in the United States of America

1 3 5 7 9 10 8 6 4 2

To the memory of Edward Said
1935–2003

After *Hamlet* and *Othello* and *King Lear* it could no longer be pretended that man was an animal who pursues pleasure and avoids pain. But of nations that pretence is still made. . . . It is not conceded that a nation should, like Hamlet, say that in its heart there was a kind of fighting that would not let it sleep, or like Othello and King Lear, hatchet its universe to ruin.

—Rebecca West, *Black Lamb and Grey Falcon: A Journey through Yugoslavia* (1942)

Contents

Preface

A suicide bomber kills nineteen—including four children—in a mixed, Jewish-Arab café, in Haifa on the eve of Yom Kippur in October 2003. While Ariel Sharon sends his planes into Syria in response, the Israeli airwaves fill with the voice of Golda Meir speaking to Israelis during the Yom Kippur War of thirty years before. In one interview, she is reported to have said that Israel had no responsibility for war "because all the wars against Israel have nothing to do with it."[1]

This book originally took shape as the Christian Gauss seminars at Princeton University in September 2003. It grew out of my desire to understand the force—at once compelling and dangerous—of Israel's dominant vision of itself as a nation. How did this vision first arise, and—apparently unanswerable—take hold? Golda Meir's view is widespread. I encountered a strong version of it from the audience at Princeton. Israel is innocent of the violence with which it is beset. There is nothing in the actions of the state, the history of the country or of Zionism, that can explain it. But even if you believe, as I do, that Zionism emerged out of the legitimate desire of a persecuted people for a homeland, the question remains. What is it about the coming into being of this nation, and the movement out of which it was born, that allowed it—that still allows it—to shed the burdens of its own history, and so flagrantly to blind itself?

Today it has become commonplace for critics of Israel responding to the charge of anti-Semitism to reply that it is Zionism, not Jewishness, which is the object of their critique. This simply displaces the problem, leads to silence. As if that were the end of the matter and nothing else remains to be said. Bizarrely, the result is that while Israel barely leaves the front page of the daily papers, Zionism itself is *hardly ever talked about*.

In the same issue of the paper reporting the words of Golda Meir, we are told of the first links being forged in the "new" postwar Iraq between Iraqi business and Israel. An "ultra- Zionist" Israeli settler has joined forces with the nephew of the now discredited Ahmad Chalabi, at one time the United States' preferred new leader of the country, to promote investment in Iraq (a venture with apparently excellent connections to the Pentagon).[2] Reading this, I shudder as I hear in my mind the anti-Semitic abuse to which such a link will give rise. But one detail draws my attention. The settler, Marc Zell, became interested in Israel in the 1980s, finally moving to the settlement of Allon Shvut in 1988 at the start of the first Palestinian intifada. It is a fact that emigration to Israel increases at times of the worst conflict (this was true of 1973 and of the settlers of the 1920s and 1930s in Palestine). Although the settlement is surrounded by barbed wire, the Zells insist that it is an ideal place for children. "It's like a small town in Iowa," they are reported to have told *Jewish Homemaker* magazine. When I visited Allon Shvut in the summer of 2002 while making a documentary on Israel and America for Channel 4 Television in England, I met Aaron and Tamara Deutsch, who had moved there from Staten Island barely a year before. They told us to admire the views as we drove away on the fortified settler roads. With bloodshed spreading across the nation, their contentment made the experience surreal. For them, too, danger was no obstacle. The land was biblically destined to be theirs, and that destiny, despite or even because of the violence, was being fulfilled.

We urgently need to understand the mind-set that runs back and forth from the Zells and the Deutsches to Golda Meir. In this book, I try to plumb some of the deep components that make up the imaginative world of Zionism. Not exhaustively—this is neither history nor survey. Of these there are now many, and indeed many brilliant, recent studies, headed by the new Israeli and Jewish historians of the past decade—Ilan Pappe, Benny Morris, Tom Segev, Avi Shlaim. My aim here is of a different kind. To try to grasp what it is about Zionism that commands such passionate and seemingly intractable allegiance. Zionism was one of the most potent collective movements of the twentieth century—on that much friends and foes of Israel will agree. But although it is one of the most powerful military nations in the world today, Israel still chooses to present itself as eternally on the defensive, as though weakness were a weapon, and vulnerability its greatest strength.

In December 2003, five teenage refuseniks, part of a growing group of young soldiers refusing to serve in the occupied territories, were jailed for a year by a Jaffa military court—the first to be court-martialed (all previous refuseniks had been given administrative sentences or allowed to go free). Summing up, the prosecutor called them "ideological criminals," "the worst kind": "the fact that they are idealistic people and in many ways positive characters should be counted against them." [3] These young men had spoken out in public; airing their disillusionment, rather than disobeying orders, appears to have been the worst offense. At moments like these, it seems that—as much as danger to its citizens—the threat to the nation, the one thing that cannot be countenanced, was collapse of conviction, or loss of belief.

In each of the chapters that follow, I track one strand in Zionism's view of the world and of its own historic task and destiny, which seems to me revelatory for where we find ourselves today. Why or how did this movement—inspired, fervent, driven by the disasters that had befallen its people—succeed, so miraculously but also so tragically, in fulfilling itself? Were the seeds of catastrophe sown somewhere at the very center of its own vision? Who were the dissenting voices? Forewarned by those in its midst, by people now mostly forgotten but who believed themselves the true Zionists, did the leaders of the movement refuse, do they still refuse, to listen? What was the effect on the fledgling nation of the fact that the genocide of the Jewish people in Europe was viewed by so many of Israel's founders as an object of shame? Can you even talk about the suffering of the Jewish people and the violence of the Israeli state in the same breath?

Against the prevalent dichotomies and false alternatives of our time, it is the wager of this book that you can, and must.

As I pursue these questions, my journey will take me to Palestine at the turn of the twentieth century and into the heart of Israel today. My cast of characters includes early visionaries for whom Zion was indeed but a dream, such as Theodor Herzl; the leaders of the nation in its very first years, Chaim Weizmann and David Ben-Gurion, who made it a reality; up to Ariel Sharon and Benjamin Netanyahu. It takes in those inside Zionism, such as Martin Buber, for whom the creation of the nation-state in 1948 was nothing short of a catastrophe, and suggests that they still have much to teach us. And it links their voices to Israel's modern internal critics: Uri Avnery, former member of the Stern gang, now leader of the campaigning peace group Gush Shalom; Naomi Chazan of Meretz, former speaker in the Knesset; novelist David Grossman; retired army general Avner Azulay; the refuseniks of the army—all of them minority and often suppressed voices whose distress at the way Israel is moving, whose relentless analysis of their country, speaks volumes about the loss of a much earlier expansive, inclusive vision of how a Jewish homeland should be.

Since I believe that Israel today is the inheritor of problems planted in its first, tentative moments, that the lines must be run both catastrophically but also more hopefully from then to now and back again, this book does not follow strict chronological time. And because I also believe that historical trauma, any trauma, takes time to surface in the minds and lives of nations and peoples, and that Jewish history has been dramatically determined by such cycles, the story, or stories, told here make their way sometimes in terrifyingly straight but also in erratic, irregular lines.

I came to this topic having been preoccupied for many years as a Jewish woman with Israel-Palestine. Having felt, most simply, repeatedly, appalled at what the Israeli nation perpetrated in my name. It will be clear from what follows that I believe the creation of Israel in 1948 led to a historic injustice against the Palestinians still awaiting redress. But at the same time, I have always felt that a simple dismissal of Zionism—as insult or dirty word—was a mistake. If something is wrong, there will be a reason for it. If it is deeply wrong, then our understanding of it will have to dig deep, force us on journeys we may not wish to take. Zionism was a vision long before it took on the mantle and often cruel powers of the modern nation-state. Being invited to Princeton provided me with the occasion to enter this history, to keep the company of Zionists who have left behind them the most extraordinary record of what they dreamed of and feared for themselves. It allowed me to delve behind the present, in the belief—confirmed in all that follows—that Zionism holds the key to the tragedy daily unfolding for both peoples in Israel-Palestine.

Over the past year while I have been completing this book, the situation has steadily deteriorated. The U.S. government, going against thirty-seven years of policy, and against international consensus, has for the first time sanctioned Israel's right to maintain settlements in the West Bank. In the face of Ariel Sharon's plan for a unilateral withdrawal from Gaza, and the construction of the separation barrier, or wall, which slices through Palestinian land and villages, the possibility of a viable Palestinian state, and hence of a two-state solution, recedes by the day. The policy of home demolitions, targeted assassination, curfew, and overall destruction of the infrastructure in the occupied territories has intensified. Transfer of the Palestinian population to neighboring Arab counties, articulated as an option by Theodor Herzl as early as 1895, is once again being openly voiced. Faced with suicide bombers, Israel demands that the Palestinians renounce terror, at the same time as, with the full backing of the United States and Great Britain, it obstructs the attempt to pursue the path of nonviolence, by refusing to recognize the authority of the International Court of Justice over the legality of the wall.[4] In July 2004, the court delivered its verdict—the wall is a political measure, unjustified on grounds of security, and a de facto land grab. When it called on Israel to take the wall down and compensate the victims, asking all signatories to the Geneva Convention to ensure its ruling be upheld, Israel refused to comply.

At the same time, a resurgence of anti-Semitism in Arab countries but also throughout Europe has become a real cause for concern. All the available information suggests that there is a link between this resurgence and the policies of the Israeli government, which does not mean, it must be loudly stated, that anti-Semitism can ever be justified. Meanwhile Ariel Sharon insists, in sentiments voiced widely inside and outside Israel, that criticism of Israel is tantamount to anti-Semitism insofar as it denies the Jewish people's right to self-defense. For many—among whom I include myself—the opposite is the case. Anti-Semitism is not caused by Israel's policies, but without a clear critique of Israel today, there is no chance of defeating it. No state can act with unlimited impunity even on grounds of self-defense. How can Jews make their appeal against anti-Semitism in the name of universal human rights unless they also speak out against the abuse of those same rights by the country that claims to represent them? This book has been undertaken in the belief that understanding why Zionism as an identity is so powerful and seemingly intransigent can also form part of such an aim.

There is another link. In the 1940s, Hannah Arendt—as she watched the new nation wrap itself in a mantle of the fiercest self-love and fear—warned that the view of anti-Semitism as eternal prevented the Jewish people from confronting it on political grounds. However real the dread, it allowed them to fence themselves off from the world. Defensive only, Zionism—already then, again today—would be unable to acknowledge itself as an active participant in the world against which it protests.

Anyone writing critically on Israel will meet the objection that Israel is being asked to be "better" than any other nation. This, it has to be said, is a claim that many Jewish writers and thinkers, as well as many Zionists of yesterday and today, appealing to a Jewish ethic, have been very happy to make for themselves. In December 2003, I was one of a group of Jewish writers who requested a meeting with the outgoing Israeli ambassador to London, Zvi Stauber, to express our fears that Israel's policies were endangering the safety of Diaspora Jewry worldwide while placing at risk the survival both of the Palestinian people and of Israel as a nation. Without prompting, he said that he did not object to double standards because he wanted there to be a "Jewish difference." For Stauber, such difference could be effortlessly folded into his apology for the state (appointed by Barak, he bridled at the suggestion that he might therefore be uncomfortable defending the policies of Ariel Sharon). In this, as we will see, he is light-years from those thinkers who, at the time of the birth of Israel, also believed that the Jewish people should be different, not as an apology for statehood, but as a warning against all the dangers into which they saw that the newly triumphant and exhilarated nation had stepped. To those who object to criticism of Israel on the grounds that it is being singled out, a question must nonetheless be put. Why is criticism of everyone else a *precondition* of criticizing Israel? (Rather than, Why is Israel being criticized *instead of* everyone else?) Isn't this argument in itself a form of exclusivity?—a plea for special protection under cover of the claim that Israel is being unfairly attacked. By what standards, then, should Israel be judged? If the standard is international law or universal rights, then the fact that other nations violate these principles is, surely, irrelevant.

Writing on Zionism is undoubtedly my way of asking Israel to be accountable for its own history. But to require a nation to take responsibility for its own actions is not the same thing as arguing that everything is that nation's fault. At Princeton, I was repeatedly asked for a critique of Arab nationalism, or more simply for greater stress on the hostility and aggression toward Israel within the Arab world. All this can be recognized without affecting my purpose here. Enduring conflicts, like the narrative of a life that has stalled, draw their energy not just from a person's—a people's—most cherished desires, but also from their no less passionately held conviction of who they are and always must be. Focusing on one side of this historic drama, the pages that follow take their cue from the psychoanalytic insight that the path to transformation lies first and foremost in knowing yourself.

July 2004

Acknowledgments

My appreciation to Princeton University and to Michael Wood for inviting me to deliver the Christian Gauss seminars in 2003. Thanks to Hal Foster for hosting them, to the university for its hospitality, to Leora Batnitzky for dialogue, to Cornel West for his last-minute interventions. I also learned much from the intensity of the audience response. Michael and Elena Wood showed me immense kindness during my stay. Mary Murrell was present throughout and I have benefited from her comments at various stages of the work. I would also like to thank Walter Lippincott for his encouragement and Fred Appel and Lauren Lepow for seeing the book with such sensitivity through the press.

A number of people have read and commented on all or part of the manuscript; although of course any remaining faults are my own, I have gained from them all—Sally Alexander, Howard Caygill, Ilan Pappe, Wadie Said, Eric Santner, Avi Shlaim. I am grateful for invitations to speak at the Psychoanalysis and History seminar organized by Sally Alexander and Barbara Taylor at London University, at the seminar in the History of Psychiatry, Psychoanalysis, Psychology and Allied Sciences in conjunction with the Psychoanalysis and History seminar as the guest of John Forrester at Cambridge University, at the Humanities Center seminar organized by Ruth Leys at Johns Hopkins University, and to deliver the London Consortium Christmas lecture as the guest of Colin MacCabe. All of these venues provided a valued forum for discussion. I continue to owe a great deal to Queen Mary University of London for creating such a stimulating intellectual environment, as well as for generously giving me the precious commodity of time. Marina Warner has offered continuous intellectual support and friendship throughout. Mia Rose tolerates my preoccupation with Israel-Palestine with immense forbearance. I thank her.

This project gained enormously from the opportunity I was given to present the documentary—*Dangerous Liaison: Israel and America*—screened on Channel 4 Television in August 2002. I am enormously grateful to David Lloyd for commissioning the program and to George Carey, Nick Read, Andy Cottam, and Fran O'Brien.

The Question of Zion is dedicated to the memory of Edward Said—its title a tribute to his 1979 *The Question of Palestine*. He would not have agreed with all of it, I am sure. But it takes its cue, at least partly, from his often overlooked insistence that Israelis and Palestinians could not coexist as two detached and separately suffering communities. His priority was justice for the Palestinians, but he also believed that there is a need, as part of this process, to understand the internal cohesion of Israel as a nation, to try to grasp what Zionism—born out of terror and exultation—meant for the Jews.

The Question of Zion

Chapter 1

"The apocalyptic sting": Zionism as Messianism (Vision)

There is a cosmic element in nationality which is its basic ingredient.

—Aaron David Gordon, "Our Tasks Ahead" (1920)

We shall discharge the great and difficult task that is laid upon us only if we are true to the great vision of the Latter Days which Israel's Prophet's foresaw and which will surely come to pass.

—David Ben-Gurion, "Science and Ethics: The Contributions of Greece, India and Israel" (1960)

Terror drives much theorisation
Into a tumult of totalisation.
Whatever the problem, Death or Passion,
One solves it in transcendental fashion.

—Gershom Scholem, "The Official Abecedarium" (to Walter Benjamin, December 5, 1927)

We have nationalised God.

—Christian Gauss, "The End of Nationalism" (1934)

Chapter 1

On December 12, 1665, Shabtai Zvi, mystical messiah, advanced on the Portuguese Synagogue in Smyrna accompanied by a motley gathering of "everyone who was in distress and trouble and all vain and light persons."[1] The rabbis, who did not believe in him, had locked the entrance, whereupon Zvi asked for an axe and hacked down the door. Once inside, he preached a blasphemous sermon, exempted the congregation from the duty of prayer, and announced that the Pentateuch was holier than the Torah; he then proceeded to appoint his first brother king of Turkey and his second emperor of Rome, and to distribute kingdoms to the various members, men and women, of the congregation.

On the following Monday, there was "great rejoicing as the Scroll of the Law was taken from the Ark"; Zvi sang songs including impure ones (Christian songs in the vernacular), declared the day his own personal Sabbath, and at night held a banquet where he distributed "money and candies" and forced all, Jews and Gentiles alike, to utter the ineffable Name.[2] This was, according to Gershom Scholem, from whose magisterial study of Zvi I take these details, the scandal that inaugurated his rule over the Jewish community of Smyrna. From the moment Shabtai Zvi was declared by Nathan of Gaza, his spiritual counselor and companion, fit to be the king of Israel, his reputation spread like wildfire across Arabia and to Europe. "Jews in Holland, England and Venice—hard-headed business men, bankers and traders," observed Chaim Weizmann—who would become Israel's first president—to the Palestine Royal Commission in Jerusalem in 1936, "gathered round this man."[3] A monstrous figure—Scholem describes him as the most hideous and uncanny figure in the whole history of Jewish messianism—Zvi fired the imaginations of the worldwide Jewish community by scandalizing supporters and opponents alike.[4] Performance artist of the forbidden, Zvi presented a paradox—not that of a saint who suffers and whose suffering is mysteriously bound to God, but that of a saint who is outrageous, a saint who sins.[5] For Scholem, who runs a line directly from Shabtai Zvi to the Zionism that is the focus of this study, this paradox is key: "A faith based on this destructive paradox has lost its innocence."[6] Destruction or even wantonness lay at the root of Zvi's capacity to inspire. The Messiah brushes, consorts with evil as much as he defeats it. Zvi exhorted his followers to blasphemy. His power rested at least partially in the relish and agony with which he appeared to violate sacred law.

As our Smyrna story tells us, Zvi also arrogated to himself the power to distribute the kingdoms of the world among women and men. He may have been divinely inspired (more later), but his reign was also firmly over this earth. Proto-Zionist, his historic task was to return the Jews to Palestine. According to Weizmann, not only did Cromwell believe in Zvi's mission, but it was this belief that lay behind his historic decision to invite the Jews to return to England (there were then no Jews in England, and it was apparently believed that the Messiah could come only when the Dispersion was complete).[7] It is central to Jewish messianism—to the consternation of official Christianity—that messianic hope is material and carnal as well as spiritual, fully embodied in political time. It must be visible, not unseen. The Jews, writes Scholem, "tended to pride themselves on this alleged shortcoming," seeing no spiritual progress in a messianic conception that announced its abdication from the sphere of history.[8] "Of the wondrous certainty of pure inwardness," characteristic of Christian belief, the Jews thought nothing: "I do not say: thought little, but thought nothing at all."[9]

In Jewish belief, history was still hovering, expectant. Redemption was public and historic, a grandiose act to be dramatized on the world's stage. Zvi's proclaimed kingship of Israel became a literally self-fulfilling prophecy. In the same year as the Smyrna scandal, reports started to spread of the arrival of the lost tribes of Israel. From Tunis it was claimed that the 1665 caravan from Mecca could not leave, as the city was besieged by the children of Israel. There is an uncanny anticipation here of Theodor Herzl, the founder of political Zionism, who expended much of his energies in futile diplomatic attempts to negotiate with the Turkish sultan. During the 1665 siege, it was reported that the sultan offered up Alexandria and Tunis to the conquerors on condition that they give up Mecca, "but they have demanded the entire Holy Land."[10]

From Sale in Morocco, the Ten Tribes of Israel were reported as appearing daily in greater and greater multitudes, about eight thousand troops covering a vast tract of ground—strangers, an unknown People whose language those who went to inquire of them "understood not."[11] An army of mythic potency, although they carry no guns—"their Arms are swords, bows, arrows and lances"—"whosoever goeth to contend with this People in Battel, are presently vanquished and slain."[12] At their head, their "Chief Leader," was a "Holy Man" who "marcheth before them, doing miracles."[13] These reports spread. Letters from Egypt referring to the appearance of the lost tribes in Arabia arrived in Amsterdam and were carried from there across Europe. When the reports from Arabia and Morocco merged, the "Arabian" army became the vanguard of an even larger Jewish army advancing from Africa. With every report the numbers grew, from tens of thousands, to three hundred thousand, to millions.

What interests me in this uncanny story—the reason why I start here—is its strange inmixing of visionary and political power. Zvi reads like an extravagant parody of inspirational man and deadly political chief. He communes deliriously with the Godhead, while hacking down the synagogue with one hand and distributing kingdoms with the other. His catastrophic radiance transmutes, almost instantaneously, into worldly authority. In a flash it empowers itself. Zvi creates a nation of multitudes out of thin air. The Ten Tribes of Israel are conquerors, invested messianically with unconditional, absolute might: "none are able to stand up against them"; "He shall cry, yea, roar, he shall prevail against his enemies."[14] When I interviewed Tamara and Aaron Deutsch at the Allon Shvut settlement outside Jerusalem in the summer of 2002 for a documentary I was presenting for Channel 4 Television in England, they told me that, although the situation in Israel had deteriorated sharply since they had arrived from Staten Island only a short eighteen months before, they nonetheless felt "invincible." I found in their dialogue the same medley of comfort and horror (comfort *in* horror) that Scholem places at the heart of one strand of apocalyptic messianism.[15] According to messianic legend, Israel—although it will ultimately be led through all tribulations to national redemption—will have to bear its share of suffering in the final cataclysm.[16] Redemption will not be realized without ruin and dread.[17] For the vision to hold, there must be slaying and being slain. "We went to visit the hospitals," the Deutsches explained; "they told us that due to this intifada . . . by blowing us up in buses and in crowded malls and wherever they might be, the birthrate has gone up dramatically."[18]

This is horror in the service of national increase (the idea of a surfeit of horror acquires a new meaning). In 1929 and 1936–39, the years of the worst Arab-Jewish confrontations in Palestine, the number of *olim*, or pioneers, among emigrants climbed, only to fall during periods of relative calm; the rate of emigration from Britain rose from 760 to 832 in the year after the Yom Kippur War, increased with the outbreak of the second intifada in 2000, and continued to climb up to 2002 (although by 2003 immigration was at its lowest level since 1989).[19] "We are," insisted the Deutsches, "happier than ever"—even though there are nights when they are "spooked" in their own homes: "You are just part of the destiny and the mystery and life."[20] Not quite exultant, certainly exhilarated. Danger, they acknowledged, was a pull: "People love reading and hearing about destruction and terror. They lap it up like there's no tomorrow."[21] Note how the vision of the apocalypse—"like there's no tomorrow"—has slipped into the common verbal coinage of the day.

Two years later, this language has in many ways become even louder and more and fervent than before. In

May 2004 Ariel Sharon's plan to evacuate the Gaza Strip and take out the settlements was defeated in a poll of his party, Likud. "If, God forbid, there is a disengagement," states Nissim Bracha of Gush Katif, one of the key settlements in Gaza designated by the plan, "I am going to destroy everything."[22] For Hagi Ben Artzi, religious Zionist and member of Gush Emunim (the Block of the Faithful), a national disaster is approaching: "And not an ordinary disaster, but in monstrous proportions—the collapse of the process of Jewish redemption."[23] To remove one settlement is to destroy not just the spiritual foundations of Zionism, not just the State of Israel, but the whole world. A minimal return of land—enacted unilaterally, without negotiation with the Palestinians, and promising nothing even vaguely close to a viable Palestinian statehood—is a violation of the Torah. Ben Artzi will commit himself to *mesirut nevesh*, or total devotion (when asked, he does not object to the analogy with the Islamic concept of martyrdom).

Catastrophe will be met with catastrophe. The word of God transcends the laws of state. "We have another partner in these decisions," Effi Eitam of the National Religious Party explained, as he threatened to withdraw from the coalition in response to Sharon's plan, "the master of the universe. We must show the master of the universe that we are willing to sacrifice our souls for the land."[24] According to one strand of Jewish thought, God's personal dignity requires the redemption of Israel. Without it, his name is profaned.[25] Ariel Sharon is guilty of defilement. Behind the rhetoric we can recognize the signs of more prosaic forms of disgust. "That this beautiful place will become the home of Arabs," states Ofra

Shoat of Bdolah (another threatened settlement in Gaza), "This is something I can't digest."[26]

These voices are not representative of the whole of Israel—far from it; more than half of the nation supported Sharon's disengagement plan. But today in Israel, catastrophe has become an identity. *Ha'aretz* feature writer Doron Rosenblum entitles a recent article "Cashing In on Catastrophe," or "how it comes about that every event and/or terrorist attack 'only proves', and even reinforces, what we already thought anyway."[27] In a cruel twist, horror, however genuinely feared, redeems Israel's view of itself.

For contemporary Jewish thinker David Hartman, founder of the Shalom Hartman Institute in Jerusalem, messianism poses the greatest threat to Israel today.[28] The nation must be brought back to earth, to the slow accommodations and political work of nonredemptive time, if it is not to destroy itself. God must be lifted out of history. With the birth of Israel, nationalism became the new messianism—the aura of the sacred, with all its glory and tribulations, passed to the state. Israel is not the only nation to believe its mandate is holy. Nor do all its citizens believe in the nation's divine sanction. For that very reason, I suggest, Israel offers us something of dramatic resonance for thinking about nationalism in the modern world: a nation vested in, at times struggling with—but repeatedly failing to discard—the mantle of God. Throughout the slow growth of Zionism as spirit and idea, messianism has cast its supernal light over the birth of Israel, "licking at the edges of its thought."[29]

According to Scholem, a line can be run from acute messianism to Zionism, but Shabtai Zvi's revolutionary messianism, and indeed the whole strand of apocalyptic messianism, have been more or less suppressed, a suppression that has robbed Judaism of one of its most creative and destructive components.[30] In the process, a key component of Zionist self-imagining has been pushed to one side, represented as extreme only, as if being in extremis, politically and cosmically, had not always been a central part of the inner formation, if not quite rationale, of the Jewish state. Part of the purpose of this first chapter will therefore be to revive the line from messianism to Zionism and carry it over to some of the secular founders of the nation who, historians of Zionism mostly insist, have nothing to do with it. In fact for Scholem, without Shabtai Zvi, there would have been no Zionist secularism, whose break with Orthodoxy was made possible only by Shabtaism's iconoclastic and anarchic "breeze"; the doctrine of the holiness of sin paved the way for indifference to all traditional Jewish law. Certainly the Orthodox opponents of early Zionism, responding to the first stirrings of the Hibbat Zion movement in the early nineteenth century, did not hesitate to make the link: "They are a new sect like that of Shabatai Zevi," pronounced the rabbi of Brisk in 1889, "may the names of evil-doers rot."[31]

At its most simple, Zionism can be understood as the first Jewish messianic movement after Zvi. This was certainly the view of Hannah Arendt, who saw Shabtaism as the "last great Jewish political activity," and the Jewish people, once the messianic hope of Shabtaism had been dashed, as essentially adrift in a world whose course no longer made sense.[32] Once it collapsed, the Jews lost, not only their faith in "a divine beginning and divine culmination of history," but also their guide "through the wilderness of bare facts."[33] Zionism can then be seen as the first movement to pick up—even more, to *revive from the dead*—this forsaken strain. In *Rome and Jerusalem*, which predates Herzl's epoch-making pamphlet *Der Judenstaat—The Jewish State* or *The Jews' State*—by more than thirty years, Moses Hess, socialist, early Zionist, claims messianism as the specific Jewish contribution to world culture: "the moment of the eternal quest, the element of permanent ferment" without which the Jews are "ghostlike," "unable to live or be revived alike."[34]

But in tracing this path, I also hope to get closer to what I see as one of the peculiarities of Zionism as a movement, a characteristic that might explain something of its compelling inner force. Horror can reside at the heart of divinity. It can give comfort, be a form of solace in an unkind, at times horrendous, world. Jewish dereliction and messianism could be seen as the two sources of Zionist discourse; or "terror" and "exultation," to use Edward Said's terms (he is discussing the need for Arab understanding of the "internal cohesion and solidity" of Israel for the Jewish people).[35] There is perhaps no more dangerous mixture for a political movement than that of being at once horrified by history and divinely inspired. From the beginning, Zionism sets out its stall on this fantasmatic terrain. "I believe," wrote J. L. Talmon—early lecturer in history at the Hebrew University of Jerusalem, in *The Nature of Jewish History*—"that Jews are to be defined as a community of fate."[36] Why is it that whatever happens, however bloody and dire, Israel always appears—at once fervently and tragically—to be somehow fulfilling itself? I include in that claim the possibility voiced recently by Daniel Barenboim and David Grossman, as well as Yaakov Perry, head of Shin Bet from 1988 to 1995, among others, that for the first time since its creation Israel might cease to exist.[37] Zionism has always felt itself under threat and often for good reason—the Arabs did not want, and many still do not want, a Jewish state in their midst. But things become more complicated if disaster is not only feared but also anticipated as part of God's plan. In the messianic view of world history, it is part of the cosmic order of things that the nation must live on a knife's edge.

This book arises for me out of an anguished curiosity. Appalled by what the Israeli state perpetrates on a daily basis in the name of the Jewish people, committed to Palestinian self-determination, or to full political and civic equality, I am nonetheless unable to follow some of the most obvious paths open to someone for whom this is the case. I am not happy, to put it at its most simple, to treat Zionism as an insult. A dirty word. Today, notably since 9/11, Zionism has, I believe, become almost impossible to talk about. "Look," insisted distinguished poet and critic Tom Paulin, "you're either a Zionist or an anti-Zionist, there's no middle way. Everyone who supports the state of Israel is a Zionist."[38] Everything hangs of course on that word "support." There is no doubt in my mind that since 9/11 Ariel Sharon has hijacked the antiterrorist agenda to impose more and more brutal policies on the occupied territories. First the "road map" and now the proposed pullout from Gaza: both appear as temporary adjustments of an utterly ruthless and consistent long-term plan. It is now clearer than ever before that this aim, with the full backing of the United States, is to render completely unviable any prospect of a Palestinian state (by Sharon's own account, it would include only 47 percent of the West Bank). Since 9/11, it has also become, if not impossible, at least much much harder in the United States, on the topic of Israel, to voice any dissent. I support neither the policies nor the silencing of critique. But "Zionist or anti-Zionist" issues a taboo. It makes of Zionism an unthinkable object. This is Georges Bensoussan opening his monumental study of the intellectual and political history of Zionism, which was published in Paris in 2002:

> The adjective [Zionist] hits out like an insult. Today the term carries such pejorative, disparaging connotations that the reality behind it has ended up disappearing under layers of stigmatization. Even, on certain international occasions, becoming diabolical. . . . But to reject Zionism, a basically atypical national ideology and movement, by stigmatizing it tells us neither what it is, nor even more what it was. Behind the exclusive focus on the Jewish-Arab conflict, the question has simply disappeared.[39]

In a strange repetition of messianism, Zionism seems to require either unconditional rejection or belief. You are Zionist or anti-Zionist. No argument. In fact inside Israel, "anti-Zionist" has a very specific meaning—it refers to those who see the project in Palestine as colonialist from the start (unlike left Zionists, for whom things began to go wrong only with the occupation of the territories that followed the 1967 Six-Day War). But there were also Zionists—Noam Chomsky was one of them in his youth—who believed that the Jews in Palestine should never acquire a sovereign state. And there were others before him, like Martin Buber, for whom the creation of the State of Israel in 1948 was, to use the term of the Palestinian refugees, a "catastrophe." Does it make any difference—can it make a difference today (the question of the second chapter)—that Zionism was from the beginning riven by internal critique?

This study therefore asks of the reader to do what may well seem impossible. To suspend both belief and disbelief. To try to enter the imaginative mind-set of Zionism in order to understand why it commands such passionate and seemingly intractable allegiance. I am convinced that a simple dismissal of Zionism fatally undermines the case it is intended to promote. On three grounds. First political. As Lenin once said, you must always construe your enemy at their strongest point. Otherwise your refusal or blindness will expose you to the enemy's unacknowledged strengths. Second, psychoanalytic. Insult an identity and you will drive it in deeper (for the same reason, you will not have any effect on Zionism by simply accusing it of being based on a set of myths). Finally, historical. Such a dismissal leaves us in complete ignorance as to what Zionism is, or was. "To paraphrase Marc Bloch to the historians of the French Revolution," Bensoussan concludes his opening paragraph, "we would like to say to the present-day protagonists: 'Zionists, anti-Zionists, for pity's sake tell us what Zionism was!' "[40]

Recent critics of Israel's policies, faced with the charge of anti-Semitism, are quick to say that their target is not

Jews but Zionism. This is not necessarily helpful. Not just because defenders of Israel's current policies will retort that the distinction is not viable if what is at stake is the right to self-defense of a Jewish nation. But more because, even where the distinction is accepted, Zionism ceases at that moment to be talked about. Or else, in an equally reductive, though largely unspoken, move, Zionism is presumed to be wholly represented by the worst activities of the state. Either way, as a divided, torn, fraught historic entity, Zionism slips back into a nightmare or a dream. Today we are often told either that the worst of Israel is the fulfillment of Zionism or that Israel today is a travesty of the true spirit of the earliest Zionist faith. Taken together these apparently contradictory views both have a kernel of truth, but either one on its own is a mistake.

Paulin is not alone in believing that between Zionism and anti-Zionism there is "no middle way." You identify or you attack—the options repeat the history of the Israeli nation-state. We can, I think, do better. I therefore want to issue a wager, or use this study to attempt an experiment. To enter the house of Zionism without blocking the exits. To try to understand what Zionism thought, at the deepest and often most disturbing level, it was doing, in its own language and terms, without cutting off the path to dissent. To use my own paraphrase of the Russian formalist Viktor Shklovsky, writing on the aesthetic options available after the Russian Revolution, "there is no third path and that is the one we are going to take."

I start on the basis that Zionism is one of the most potent collective movements of the twentieth century, whose potency needs urgently to be understood. It has the capacity to foster identifications that are as immutable as, indeed, the ineffable Name. As a movement, Zionism has the power, that is, to sacralize itself. For its supporters that is of course its divinely sanctioned purpose and strength. For its detractors, that is the delusion on which the destructiveness of the present-day Israeli state most fundamentally rests. But to call something a delusion does not satisfy me. Something can be both a delusion and actual; effective and insane. In a famous exchange with Jung, Freud insisted that when patients are preoccupied with their childhood, there is no point in the analyst's objecting that their obsession is evasive or illusory, a turning away from the tasks of adult life. For even were this true, if you say as much, you will merely provoke the fiercest resistance. People are stubborn in their beliefs. States of conviction, drawing their force from the depths of the soul and of history, brook no argument. Shabtaism was nothing if not obdurate. Even when Zvi committed apostasy by converting to Islam, the worst betrayal, many of his followers remained undeterred. "Enthusiasm and love know of no hopeless situations," writes Renan on the Christian apostles when their hopes of redemption had been dashed. Scholem cites him with reference to Zvi: "They play with the impossible, and rather than despair, they violate reality."[41]

Violating reality is something that more than one Zionist has been perfectly happy to acknowledge that they do. The famous epigraph to Theodor Herzl's 1902 novel *Altneuland* reads, "If you will, it is no fairy tale."[42] In the epilogue the narrator addresses his book as a child:

"[Your father] believes that dreaming is as good a way to spend your time on earth as any other, and dream and action are not so far apart as is often thought. All the activity of mankind was a dream once and will again be a dream."[43] In fact this could be seen as a sacrilege, as it suggests Israel might revert to a dream. But Zionism is a movement that foregrounds its own fantasmatic dimension. Against its own shibboleth—"a land without a people for a people without a land'—it always knew it was propelling itself into an imaginary and perhaps unrealizable space. Before anything else, Zionism presents itself as a movement of hope and desire, with no necessary purchase on the ground that it would finally summon beneath its feet. To be a Zionist, Chaim Weizmann comments in 1909, "it was not necessary, in the first place, to be convinced that the idea could be carried out."[44] "We have to create our title out of our wish to go to Palestine" (perhaps the clearest, most politically frank version of what Freud will term magical thinking or omnipotence of thoughts).[45] In 1903 Weizmann had written to Gregory Lurie, "[A]s a concrete proposition, [Palestine] does not even come within our comprehension."[46] Zionism presents us with a political movement that appears to be at once unanswerable and unreal. Freud's (or Jung's) patient does not know he is deluded. But Zionism, as we will see, is a violation of reality that knows its own delusion. And runs with it.

Let's begin therefore—it is the basic axiom of psychoanalysis—by respecting the symptom. "It is the Zionist's good fortune," declared Chaim Weizmann at a Zionist meeting in Paris in 1914, "that they are considered mad; if we were normal, we would not consider going to Palestine but stay put like all normal people."[47] We are therefore doing no more than following the first president of the State of Israel if we take Zionism to be a form of collective insanity. But with this caveat: that there is no sanity when it comes to the ethos of the group. "The diagnosis of communal neurosis," Freud writes, "is faced with special difficulty." "In an individual neurosis we take as our starting-point the contrast that distinguishes the patient from his environment, which is assumed to be 'normal'."[48] But for a group "all of whose members are affected by one and the same disorder no such background could exist."[49] There is no normal yardstick by which we can measure the neurosis of the group. All-absorbing, a group is its own environment, creates its own world. If group identifications are so lethal, it is because they swallow up their own reserve. Freud comes very close—other analysts will get closer—to stating that groups are mad. By definition.

It is the characteristic of most groups that boundaries melt on the inside (members of a group become as one), harden—arm themselves—all around the edge. To return to Shabtai Zvi: no enemy will survive in combat against Israel, but inside the circle of the chosen, or at least in the person of the Messiah, the barriers scandalously crumble between man and the divine. Into his own person and history, Zvi draws the wild, dark core that subsists at the heart of the collective passion called Zionism.

Messianism flourishes in dark times. Like Zionism, it is the child of exile. "In the history of Judaism," writes Scholem, the influence of messianism "has been exercised almost exclusively under the conditions of the exile as a primary reality of Jewish life and of Jewish history."[50] Delivering his address to the Jubilee of the First Zionist Congress in Basel in August 1947, Chaim Weizmann described how Theodor Herzl's *Der Judenstaat* immediately won the hearts of the Jewish masses because it appeared at a moment when the horizon for Russian Polish Jewry was looking so bleak: "There was something messianic in it. . . . At times like these there is always a recrudescence of messianic hope"—he was speaking in the year of the UN charter for a partitioned Palestine.[51] In January 1940, in the thick of the war, which can fairly be described as the darkest time, Weizmann had addressed a crowd estimated at six thousand at the Mecca Temple in New York: "The path we are treading is very hard indeed. It now looks almost like the travails before redemption."[52]

Shabtaism itself arose, as Scholem stresses, in the aftermath of the Chiemnilitski massacre in Poland in 1648 when a petty officer of the Ukrainian forces united with the Cossacks and went on a marauding expedition into the country slaughtering the Jews; the gloom and sense of hopelessness weighing down the next generation in Poland provided a rich breeding ground for mystical and messianic hopes.[53] Chiemnilitski would pass into folklore—a crucial part of Jewish collective consciousness, it is still referred to by Israeli leaders today. Nor was it only the disasters of the Polish Jews that inspired messianic hope. Spectacular rises to prosperity in the Jewish community of the Diaspora were seen as no less a reason for anxiety. Nothing crystallized, nothing held. In the face of such instability, writings laced with the eschatological mood of the age were eagerly read throughout the Jewish world.[54]

Up to 1492, the messianic strand of Judaism had waned, but after the expulsion, the exiles from Spain responded "with a wave of apocalyptic agitation," "messianic birth pangs" that would eventually reach their apotheosis in the life and movement of Shabtai Zvi.[55] Redemption arises on the ruins of history. Disaster must be meaningful if it is to be borne. "The bitter experience of many generations that had tasted the heavy yoke of alien rule, oppression and humiliation," writes Scholem, "was not likely to mitigate the violence of this type of eschatology, whose roots go back to the apocalyptic literature of the period of the Second Temple."[56] Messianic legend drenches itself in "uninhibited fantasies" about the catastrophic aspects of redemption. Born of catastrophe, it promises more. "Jewish Messianism is in its origins and by its nature," writes Scholem, "a theory of catastrophe. . . . *This cannot be sufficiently emphasised.*"[57] When Maimonides tried to abolish messianism as a historical force—indeed, retracing this path, David Hartman invokes Maimonides in making his appeal against the messianism of Israel today—early sixteenth-century Jewish writers, such as Don Isaac Abravanel and R. Loew of Prague, taking their cue from the expulsion, responded by bringing its catastrophic dimension once again to the fore. In the apocalyptic imagination, comfort and horror had an equal share, allowing a persecuted and downtrodden people to balance "many a bitter account with its torturers."[58] Messianic redemption is therefore a form of historic revenge. To put it crudely, it is a way of settling scores. The violence of a cruel history repeats itself as its own cure.

There is a paradox here. It was misery that drew the Jewish people to the apocalyptic tradition and its message of catastrophe. But as they move forward to the dawn of a new history, the misery accompanies the vision, lodges itself inexorably inside the dream. The future that is meant to redeem you borrows the most dreaded trait of the past. However utopian the hopes, the worst will not let go (it carries over like a demented, never-ending mathematical game).

According to an opinion poll in 2002, more than 80 percent of Israelis wanted a peace deal with the Palestinians; more than 80 percent supported Sharon's brutal policies of reoccupation of Gaza and the West Bank, policies that have since intensified in Gaza as a preliminary to the planned withdrawal which may or may not take place. Try doing the figures. They don't add up. Two years later, at the 150,000-strong demonstration in support of the Gaza pullout plan in May 2004, not one criticism was voiced of the army's destruction of Rafah that was going on at the same time, nor, by prior agreement, was anyone refusing to serve in the army allowed to speak: " 'Something must be done' always goes in two directions," writes poet Yitzhak Laor. "The first leads to the demonstration square (and then back home). The second leads to the military operation that has just won ecstatic support."[59] As if catastrophic exultation, alongside the desire for a resolution to the conflict, had worked itself into the national mind. To which must be added the fact that the pullout is likely to precipitate anything but peace, given that it is attached to the unilateral annexation of roughly 50 percent of the West Bank. We are, wrote Uri Avnery—former Knesset member, now one of Israel's most vocal critics—in one of his *Gush-Shalom* dispatches, a schizophrenic country.[60] There must be violence. There must be peace. As a phrase, "the cycle of violence"—to use one of the clichés of the region—might be more apt than we think. How on earth can you stop something whose meaning stretches back through the annals of history and forward to the ends of time?

Like an individual in thrall to his passion, his perversity, and his symptom, a nation can be both self-defeating and unerring in its aim. But if it is relatively easy to acknowledge this of individuals, it is far more shocking to consider that a nation, apparently inspired, believing fervently in its own goodness in the world, might be devoted not only to the destruction of others but to sabotaging itself. Of nations, writes Rebecca West in the epigraph to this book, the pretense is still made that man is an animal who pursues pleasure and avoids pain. We find it hard to believe that in the heart of a nation there could be a kind of fighting that will not let it sleep, or that might hatchet its universe to ruin. For Scholem, reviving the most demonic components of the Jewish mystical tradition to which he devoted his life's work, something difficult and often bitter had been silenced. It needed to be invoked once more—he wrote his study in the 1940s in Jerusalem when all around him the national future of the Jews was taking shape—for the contemporary state of the Jewish people to be understood. Can Israel live a life that is "not ideal, not demonic"?—the question of writer David Grossman, also writing out of Jerusalem half a century later, more or less in despair.[61]

One of Scholem's main tasks is to demonstrate the way that Jewish mysticism, notably in the Lurianic version which directly precedes the life and times of Shabtai Zvi, carries the seeds of what was historically to come. He is struggling to show that mysticism plays its part in the evolution of the Jewish people as more than a strange aberrant form of thought. If the Lurianic Kabbalah, developed in Safed in the middle of the sixteenth century, is crucial, it is because it was through its influence that Jewish mysticism became part of the general, public, consciousness of Jewish life. Lurianism was mythological, a rendering of divine acts and events that translate effortlessly into the sphere of history. Thus it was central to Lurianic mysticism that God could manifest himself only because he had first withdrawn or contracted himself.[62] Right inside the spiritual process, we find a perfect analogy for exile: God becomes, like his chosen people, "an exile into Himself."[63] According to the Talmud, wherever Israel is exiled, the divine source or Shekinah goes with it. In Lurianic kabbalism, man has been in exile ever since the "breaking of the vessels," when the supernal light emanating from the divine source shattered the vessels waiting to contain it. Whereupon fragments, together with the divine sparks attached to them, were released into primordial space. From that point on, nothing was in its rightful and appointed place. The world is out of joint. The task of restitution or *tikkun*, of gathering the scattered fragments, then falls to man.

With the "breaking of the vessels," writes Scholem, "the historical notion of exile had become a cosmic symbol."[64] This makes historic destitution supremely meaningful, lifts tragedy out of the dust. The perfect philosophy of exile, messianism allows the Jews to view themselves, not as historical indigents and ciphers, but as a major force in history.[65] For a generation in exile, whose precarious existence was a "most pressing and cruel problem," it was the perfect answer.[66] Exile and redemption were illuminated, and the "unique historical situation of Israel" becomes symbolic of "the state of creation as a whole."[67] Palestine is elevated to cosmic stature: "What we have come to find in Palestine," writes Aaron David Gordon, whose writings set the tone for a whole early generation of Labor Zionists and from whom my opening epigraph for this chapter is taken, "is the cosmic element." (Hertzberg describes Gordon as Labor Zionism's "secular mystic and saint.")[68] Fueled by the historic needs of the Jewish people, on the verge of seizing its own patch of ground, Zionism raises itself to the heavens: "The anticipation of redemption is the force which keeps exilic Judaism alive, and the Judaism of the land of Israel is salvation itself"—the words of Abraham Isaac Kook, first chief rabbi of Palestine, mentor of Israel's redemptive-religious wing, and inspiration for many Israelis today.[69]

According to kabbalistic legend, Adam—whose task was that of the first redeemer—had failed. Tearing asunder what was already joined, he had "destroyed the plantations."[70] The land must therefore be restored—we can already see here a glimpse of Israel's mythos of redeeming, planting, the earth. When the Messiah comes and the Jews arrive in Palestine, the whole cosmos, not just Israel, will therefore be set to rights. "The exile of

Israel and the destruction of our Temple are an [anomalous] exception to the order of the universe," proclaimed R. Loew, writing after the exile, "and an exception only has temporary existence."[71] It is as if, almost paradoxically, Zionism can be ruthless because it is saving far more than the Jews. In the words of Rabbi Kook, "all the civilisations of the world will be renewed by the renascence of our spirit. All religions will don new and precious raiments, casting off whatever is soiled, abominable, unclean."[72] "Our soul encompasses the entire universe, and represents it in its highest unity."[73]

Janus-faced, Zionism therefore turns toward cosmic and historical time. Without this latent duality, the force of Zionism as an identity cannot, I believe, be fully understood. Throughout his account of Jewish mysticism, Scholem stresses how an internal spiritual path—obedience to the Torah—is fueled by and fuels the Jewish narrative of historic catastrophe. In the first instance, messianism is spiritual, internal. The early Kabbalists' concern was with the mystical meaning of the redemption. Yet the facts of Jewish history place the exclusively spiritual dimension of *tikkun* under increasing strain. Lurianism was also always a powerful national myth, and its fervent vision of an end to degradation contained, explosively at its core, the violent messianic potential that erupted in Shabtaism. To spark this conflagration needed only a match. To make the transit from metaphoric to historic journey, from redemption of the soul to redemption of the people, from spiritual path to mass movement, eschatological thinking had to cross only the finest line. "The eruption of the volcano, when it came, was terrific."[74] Now the Messiah would redeem the people and Israel would fulfill its destiny in the world. Zvi's mentor, interlocutor, and interpreter, Nathan of Gaza, was explicit that evil was at once mystical and political. The forces of evil were present not only in the demonic powers of the Kabbalah, but also in the rule of tyranny on earth, in the profane history of the world, and in "Israel's exile among 'Edom' and 'Ishmael'."[75] Even for those like Maimonides who rejected messianism in its acute form, the only difference between this aeon and the days of the Messiah was "the subjection [of Israel] to the nations."[76]

Massively overdetermined as a concept, *tikkun* (mending, restoration, reintegration) is therefore called upon to do a great deal of psychic and political work: restoring the Godhead to itself; returning the people of Israel to Palestine; and—in one version of Zionism, which sees itself as redemptive, not just for the Jews, but for all of humanity—gathering the scattered fragments, the divine sparks, of the vessels that have shattered across the face of the whole world. What, it seems fair to ask, is the price of the cosmic destiny with which the nation has burdened itself? The judgment on the non-Jew at least is clear. The Gentile nations have abandoned the task entrusted to Adam; their souls stem from the sphere of evil. Only the Jews can redeem the dross of the world.[77]

Shabtai Zvi adds another crucial twist to this drama. Remember that he performed strange acts, violating holy law. In the wings of inspiration, outrage awaits its cue. Something shocking is about to happen. As if those claiming access to divinity are always on the point of being appalled by themselves. For Nathan of Gaza, the strange and wonderful acts performed by Zvi proved his authenticity. On the face of it, Zvi's apostasy, his conversion to Islam, was the utmost betrayal: unredeemable, we might say. But not so. The catastrophic harbingers of redemption widen to include, not only wars, famine, pestilence, but apostasy and the desecration of God's name. Go back to Lurianic mysticism, and Zvi's most scandalous act becomes part of the redemptive plan. When the divine sparks fell into the world, the Messiah fell with them. It was the task of the Messiah, and only his, to redescend into evil in order to open the gates of the prison from within: "Just as the Shekinah had to descend to Egypt—the symbol of everything dark and demonic [*sic*]—to gather in the fallen sparks, so the Messiah too at the end of the ages starts on his most difficult journey to the empire of darkness, in order to complete his mission" (Zvi's sojourn with the Turks was compared to Moses's time at the court of the pharaoh).[78] The ultimate messianic task becomes not merely to defeat and annihilate the power of evil, but to raise it up to the sphere of holiness. Man must descend into evil in order to redeem himself: "When you have sunk to the lowest level," God says to Israel, "at that time I will redeem you."[79]

If this is the case, then the process of restitution can no longer be advanced by pious acts. Evil must be fought with evil—"In order to fulfil his mission, he must condemn himself through his own acts."[80] In the words of Nathan of Gaza, you must loose the knots of the demonic powers in order to make wars against them (or as Freud would put it, you must catch your thief in order to hang him). Zvi will subdue the pharaoh, but he also *is* the pharaoh.[81] At one level, Scholem presents us with a Messiah struggling against the demonic components of his inner self, as if Zvi was himself, or contained in his innermost being, the very principle that he is trying to subdue. "It is difficult," Scholem muses, "to escape wondering about the prefiguration of some very modern psychoanalytic ideas in these paradoxical theses of kabbalistic psychology."[82] Either way, from this point on, evil lay on the path to redemption. The conversion of Shabtai Zvi would hover in historical memory as an appalling and inspiring reminder that "Good and Evil were the two paths open to the people of Israel on their way to Redemption."[83]

It is hard not to find in these strange, twisted concepts—which for Scholem are the very heart of the matter—a resonance for our modern times. A recognition, all too fleeting, that evil might be an internal matter, immediately disposed of in the cosmic struggle to annihilate it. And an uncanny echo, not just of some of the present-day rhetoric of the Israeli state, but of the whole language of retributive justice, backed by a fervent belief in the morality of divinely sanctioned awfulness, which has been so central to public discourse since 9/11. We live in a time when the means of combating "evil" seem to take on the colors of what they are trying to defeat. Fundamentalism—this may be the simplest point to make here—is not just an Islamic affair. Radical Shabtaian Joseph Frank was known to cite the famous phrase attributed by the Gnostics to Jesus, that the path to redemption consists of "treading upon the vesture of shame."[84] If this is for Scholem a depraved, nihilistic mysticism, it nonetheless contains an edifying paradox. The fight against evil knows no limits. Shame can be its own servant. Catastrophe can become a passion. Trauma repeats itself. Emotional identification trumps reality. Violent euphoria, even when bitterly disappointed by history, acquires its own afterlife. For those who "refused to accept the verdict of history," the psychological by-products of Shabtaism acquired "an autonomous life of their own."[85]

It is my argument here that messianism colors Zionism, including secular Zionism, at every turn. In *Trial and Error*, Weizmann describes his earliest Zionist urges as a young boy in Pinsk. Before "practical nationalism" assumed its form, "the 'Return' was in the air, a vague deep-rooted Messianism, a hope which would not die."[86] One *Rebbi* (teacher), he recounts, who considered it "impious and presumptuous" for any youngster "to so much as mention the rebuilding of Palestine," admonished him to keep quiet: "*You'll* never bring the Messiah any nearer. One has to do much, learn much, know much and suffer much before one is worthy of that."[87] Weizmann is silenced, but like any forbidden object, the image of a messianic fulfillment continues, even more forcefully, to do its work in his mind. Weizmann is only one of several to ascribe to Theodor Herzl something like messianic powers. "He glowed—at the time radium was not known—with a kind of Zionist radio-activity, electrifying his entire environment."[88] Martin Buber described Herzl as bearing a "countenance with the glance of the Messiah."[89] Herzl's biographer Amos Elon describes him as following a line of "bizarre dreamers, gamblers, adventurers and audacious showmen which one had assumed had ended with Cagliostro or Sabbatai Zevi."[90] In June 1895, Herzl showed his manuscript to Friedrich Schiff, the Parisian correspondent of the Wolff telegraphic agency: "Schiff says: it is a thing someone tried to accomplish in the last century—Sabbatai! Well, in the last century it was impossible. Now it is possible—because we have machines."[91] Later he qualified: "The difference between myself and Sabbatai Zevi (the way I imagine him) . . . is that Sabbatai made himself great to be the equal of the great of the earth. I however find the great small, as small as myself."[92]

The modesty was not sustained. "I believe," Herzl wrote in a diary entry on the completion of *Der Judenstaat*, "for me life has ended and world history has begun."[93] "I bring you salvation," he declared in a speech to the Rothschilds in 1895.[94] To his first biographer Reuben Brainin in 1919, he described this dream he had had at the age of twelve:

> [The Messiah] took me in his arms and carried me off on wings of heaven. On one of the iridescent clouds we met . . . Moses. . . . The Messiah called out to Moses, "For this child I have prayed!" To me he said, "Go and announce to the Jews that I shall soon come and perform great and wondrous deeds for my people and all mankind!"

For many years, Herzl kept this dream to himself "and did not dare tell anyone."[95]

Herzl shares with Shabtai Zvi a creative mania that is at the core of their inspiration (it is impossible to read Scholem on Zvi alongside Amos Elon, Herzl's biographer, without being struck by the similarities between the two men). Repeatedly Scholem insists that Zvi went to Nathan of Gaza not because he believed he was the Messiah but as a sick man in search of a doctor of the soul. Zvi, we could say, needed Nathan of Gaza to release his own desire. This brings the origins of Shabtaism close, roughly three centuries before its time, to a psychoanalytic cure. In a scene oddly similar to the moments when Freud faints in the company of Jung, Nathan of Gaza is reported to have proclaimed Zvi fit to be king of Israel after falling into a swoon (Herzl also suffered from brain anemia and blackouts). Scholem diagnosed Zvi as suffering manic-depressive psychosis combined with paranoid traits. But you do not have to accept this diagnosis, nor indeed his often impatient view of Zvi as displaying depressing passivity or as autistically centered on himself, to recognize in both these larger-than-life historical characters—Zvi and Herzl—all the features of the divine fool. In the words of Sufi mystic al-Junayd cited by Scholem, "God brings upon those that love him a kind of sudden and supernatural madness."[96]

In one of his most delirious fantasies, Herzl envisaged transporting entire centers of Judaism to be dug out and transplanted from the Old World to the New. A huge construct like the Palais Royal or St. Mark's in Venice would be built where, in awesome ceremony, his father would be made first senator, his son doge (not without echoes of Zvi dispensing powers in the synagogue).[97] He himself was to place the crown on the head of "Your highness—my beloved son."[98] When Herzl ends a letter to his wife with the greeting for his son "Gentle kisses to my Vaterkönig," Elon comments: "A mystifying term. Perhaps a family joke. Perhaps it echoes *Avinu*

Malkenu (in Hebrew, 'our father-king'), the appellation of God in the Hebrew prayer."[99]

These fantasies may have been intimate, private, buried, but that does not have to detract from their effect. More than charismatic, Herzl had inspirational powers. Weizmann insists that it was not his ideas—"*The Jewish State* contained not a single new idea"—but the fervor of his belief, the radiation of his personality, that gave Herzl his authority.[100] As with Zvi, to whom Elon compares him, Herzl's fervor inspired his followers with a vision of redemption. In 1896, at a mass meeting in Sofia, when Weizmann saw him for the first time, the chief rabbi proclaimed him the Messiah. "Perhaps," suggested Moritz Güdemann, chief rabbi of Vienna, who would later turn against Zionism, "you are the one called of God."[101] For days after Herzl's funeral, an eighteen-year-old Ben-Gurion was overcome with grief: "Today more than ever I believe we shall succeed. I know the day will come—it is not far—when we return to the wonderful land, the land of truth and poetry, of roses and prophetic visions."[102] By the end of his life, Herzl himself had become more cautious: "Our people believe that I am the Messiah. I myself do not know this, for I am no theologian."[103]

There are, however, some important distinctions to be made. The suggestion that Zionism is—at least in one key current—a form of messianism, would by no means receive universal assent. For the ultra-Orthodox, Zionism was a revolt against God, a religious sin of the first degree. For a number of groups, Naturei Karta, Satmar

Hasidim, and the Edah Herudit of Jerusalem, Zionism is demonic, an eruption of antimessianic force. By seizing the initiative from history, Zionism violates messianic expectation, thrusting the task of redemption, in an act of pure sacrilege, into the hands of Man—in a modern formulation of Naturei Karta: "*a pollution that encompasses all other pollutions . . . a heresy that includes all other heresies.*"[104] Zionism usurps the divine prerogative. In the minds of the Orthodox, it violates the three sacred oaths central to messianic belief: not to ascend the wall (Israel must not burst into the land as one); not to force the end (to be left in the hands of heaven); not to rebel against the nations (there must be no countering the will of the world). In the biblical texts that served to crystallize the messianic idea in the minds of many—Amos's Day of the Lord, Isaiah's vision of the end of days—human activity is redundant. It degrades God's redemptive purpose to make it dependent on the will or conduct of man.

In the mind of these radical anti-Zionists, true messianism is expectant, passive. For that very reason, secular Zionists have always worked hard to disintricate Zionism from messianism. "For [the Zionist intelligentsia]," writes Bensoussan, "the preaching of the *maggidim* would trap the population in the passive expectation of the 'Saviour', whether he be called Sabbatai Zvi or Theodor Herzl."[105] Secular Zionism is active—"muscular" in one account—engaged in the tasks of the world. In the minds of many of these early Zionists, the religious concept of redemption was trapped in the image of Jewish helplessness. Yet again the Jews were expected to do nothing for—or to save—themselves. To be active meant shedding the messianic dream, stripping away its deleterious fantasy, to free the space for "concrete activity in the here and now."[106]

It was therefore the aim of these first pioneers of secular Zionism to purge the national endeavor of the cosmic mythos with which it seemed so readily to imbue itself. "The new Zionism which has been called political," writes Max Nordau—Herzl's most important disciple and colleague—in his essay "Zionism" of 1902, "differs from the old, religious, messianic variety in that it disavows all mysticism, no longer identifies with messianism."[107] Secular Zionism's revolution was to move salvation from the heaven to the plains: "[it] does not expect the return to Palestine to be brought about by a miracle, but desires to prepare the way by its own efforts."[108]

But traces of messianic redemption, even in its acute form, can be found in the language of those who in many ways struggled hardest to defeat it. So much so that we can fairly ask whether the affinity between Zionism and messianism is too intimate and powerful to have ever been anything other than partially—and finally unsuccessfully—repressed. At the First Zionist Congress in 1897, Herzl had felt the need to insist that Zionism was not "a kind of chiliastic horror."[109] For one critic of Scholem, objecting to his affiliation with Brit Shalom, political Zionism, not Judaism, was the truest heir of messianic hope: "Our historical messianic hope exists even today in the heart of the new Israeli man in the form of political Zionism in a much more complete way than the messianic idea existed in the past in the heart of the religious Jew" (he was objecting to Brit Shalom's support for equal political rights for Arab and Jew as inhibiting the full redemption of the Jewish people).[110]

Recent commentators—Aviezer Ravitsky, Ehud Sprinzak, Eliezer Shweid, Ian Lustick—are in agreement that the attempt to effect a radical break between Zionism and messianism, or between secular and religious Zionism, has failed.[111] And in a sense always did. Israel has never succeeded in distinguishing between action in the sphere of history and hopes that at once fulfill history and leave its world behind. "Believing that a Jew could hold a purely secular vision of Palestine," writes Bensoussan, "is, in the words of Marx, to forget the weight of the dead on the brains of the living."[112] Even if only unconsciously, there was always an apocalyptic desire to wipe out the old aeon of exile and suffering, even among the socialist pioneers.[113] For the early secular Zionists, the Bible still remained the foundational text—it did not have to be the word of God to retain its power to shape the personal and national identity of the Jew.[114] You can see it in the very name of the nation, replete with the theological meanings of "Kingdom of Israel" and "Congregation of Israel" on high. Whatever was in the minds of the members of the National Council, as they gathered to consider how to name the Jewish state on the eve of the 1948 proclamation, they cast the aura of divine sanction over the fledgling nation.[115]

Zionism is not of course alone in imbuing nationalism with a messianic strain—nationalism always contains a fervent drive to actualization somewhere at the core. Mazzini had also dreamed of Rome as the center of a new world (in *Rome and Jerusalem*, Moses Hess simply transfers the center of messianic fulfillment to Jerusalem from Rome). But Zionism is unique in laying one by one the terms of messianic destiny, lifted from a Jewish faith, across its geographical landscape even when that faith had been lost. "Too many elements in Zionist activity and rhetoric evoked the classical vision of redemption," Ravitsky writes in *Messianism, Zionism and Jewish Religious Radicalism*, "for a view that unwaveringly distinguished between the two to capture people's imaginations for long":

> Zionism called for Jewish immigration to the Land of Israel just as messianism promised the return to Zion and the ingathering of the exiles. As the former movement sought to attain political independence for the Jewish people, the latter hoped for the liberation of the Jews from "subjugation to the great powers." Zionism worked to make the land fruitful, to "conquer the waste places"; it even spoke explicitly of "redeeming the land." Employing a somewhat different idiom, messianism taught (in the words of the Talmud) that "there is no revealed End than this, as it is said, 'But you, O mountains of Israel, shall yield your produce and bear your fruit, for their return is near.' "[116]

Today, as we have already seen, the language of redemption is voiced most loudly by Gush Emunim, the movement for the promotion of Jewish settlement in Eretz Israel: "Ours is not an autonomous scale of values, the product of human reason, but rather a heteronomous or, more correctly, 'theonomous' scale rooted in the will of the Divine architect of the universe and its moral order."[117] Or more simply: "We have another partner in these decisions. We must show the master of the universe that we are willing to sacrifice our souls for the land."

Although by no means a mass movement, Gush Emunim exert considerable influence. Their ideas are fully or partially represented in the Israeli parliament by the National Religious Party, Moledet, Tzomet, and many members of Likud. More recently it has been estimated that their views are tolerated by more than 50 percent of those who vote for the religious parties. Menachim Begin, Likud's first leader, used to refer to them as "my dear children"—they have also been described as the "kibbutz" movement of the entire Israeli Right.[118] When members of Gush Emunim engaged in acts of anti-Arab violence, notably in response to the first intifada, they were often found to be highly trained officers and soldiers in reserve in the Israeli army.

For Gush Emunim, the victory of the Six-Day War was divinely ordained (for those inside Israel today who define themselves as "left Zionists," this misplaced messianic fervor attached to the war is the watershed). Any travesty of the conquest is a violation of the will of God. The turning point was 1973, when their belief in redemption was blighted by the humiliation, and what has passed into history as the near-defeat, of the army in the Yom Kippur War. Henceforth they saw themselves even more as the protectors of Israel's refusal to compromise itself. In 1982, responding to the final implementation of the 1979 Camp David accord to return Sinai to Egypt in return for peace, two of their members, convinced that such a historical setback required an equivalent act of desecration, planned, in a gesture of messianic violence, to blow up the Muslim Dome of the Rock.

Gush Emunim are the most vocal heirs of Rabbi Kook, for whom the State of Israel was to be the foundation of

God's presence in the world (although they are not as far to the right as the officially banned, violently messianic movement of Kach). As self-appointed guardians of the settlements, they could be said to hold, not just the future, but the soul of the nation in their hands. If they seem somehow marginal, despite their tacit support across the nation, they nonetheless play a crucial psychological and political part in the national drama of redemption. It is as if the nation had tacitly agreed to bestow on them the legacy of its most violent messianic hopes—treating them rather like a mentally troubled member of the family, at once benignly tolerated and disowned, who allows it to carry on as if everything were normal by bearing the weight of the ugliest secrets of the whole group.

For that very reason, it is not this strand that should interest us most. By making so much noise, it distracts attention from the more subtle currents of messianism in Israel's prehistory and its national life. Go back to the nineteenth century: some of the earliest Zionists, the Harbingers as they are known—Yehudah Alkalai and Zvi Kalischer—saw their task in strictly messianic terms (they open Arthur Hertzberg's collection as the "precursors"). It was Alkalai and Kalischer who defined messianism as worldly task, stirring up messianic elements that had long lain dormant, "causing the ancient seeds of activism to germinate and grow."[119] In many ways they were children of modernity, having been inspired to a belief in such benign historical action by the emancipation of the European Jews—by making the Jews a people, Zionism would go one stage further in fulfilling the messianic task of modern times. One by one they answered each of the sacred charges against a return to the land of Palestine: there would be no usurping of the divine task since they were only making the ground ready "for a descent of the Divine presence among us."[120] The miraculous, utopian end would be left in the hands of heaven. And there would be no forcing, as the effort would be modest—"little by little"—and slow: "we shall have to build houses, dig wells, and plant vines and olive trees"—the very activity and of course also whole ethos of the first secular pioneers.[121] How could human activity interfere with God's purpose if such activity is—as it always is—imperfect, transient, incomplete? Nor would the process counter the will of the nations, as the return would be political, not military, carried out with universal assent.

This is slow redemption, shorn of its catastrophic element. Today we can see the Harbingers as attempting the most delicate of experiments—to wrest Zionism from its own latent violence (no conflict), to give to the earliest stirrings of settlement in Palestine a vision of the world at once redemptive, normative, sane. Hartman tells the story of his first visit to a religious kibbutz, when he was taken aside by one of its founders to see, not his library of rare books, but a tree: " 'What a transformation of consciousness,' I thought. Not his books but his tree, the work of his hands. For me this was truly a sign of the success of the Zionist quest for normalcy."[122]

In this earliest, gradualist, Zionism, messianism therefore takes root in the earth. It lands. For A. D. Gordon, who would be a major influence on David Ben-Gurion, the land of Palestine was sacred, labor a religious task, nationhood cosmic. In the Kabbalah, the divine effluence pours down from the supernal spheres of the spirit into the grim natural world. For Gordon, it wells up from the earth: "each of . . . the powers of the soul has a different luminosity here, a different colouring, a different richness, a different profundity, a different clarity and a different mystery from that which it had in those other lands."[123] "I love all the land of Israel," states Gideon Naor of the settlement Kfar Darom, the first in Gaza and now marked for evacuation under Sharon's plan. "In every material thing, there is something spiritual. In a fruit that grew in the land of Israel, there is holiness."[124]

By cleaving to the land, man cleaves to the Divine. For Gordon, if the Jews have a deed to the land of Israel, it is not because the land is promised in the Bible, "but because it was in the land of Israel that the Bible was created."[125] The Bible is therefore testimony to the creative potential of the land. By transforming the land, man fulfills this potential, sets the world (and himself) on the celestial path. For Rabbi Kook, the land of Palestine is holy in and of itself; for Gordon only labor redeems—slowly, incrementally, by the work of hands. Gordon's term was *Avodah*, which combined labor with the older meaning of service to God. If Kook's objective is a Torah State, for Gordon it is closer to a worker's cooperative.[126] The significance of the land is embodied in the substance and contours of the land itself. To put it at its most simple, you had to be there. It is impossible to overestimate how crucial this apparently benign ethos will come to be in justifying the Jewish claim to Palestine: "We think," Weizmann states in his address to the Palestine Royal Commission in Jerusalem in 1936, "that you possess a thing only when you build it with your own hands."[127]

If we return now to Scholem, we find this secular vision of national redemption already figured in one version of restitution, or *tikkun*. In fact it was always a question for messianism whether the redemption would come first and then the world would be transformed, or whether transformation on earth was the prerequisite—precisely the preliminary stage—for the redeemer to come. It becomes much harder to wrest secular Zionism from its messianic roots once we recognize that for one interpretation of Kabbalah, human activity has a crucial role, if not *the* crucial role, to play in the purification of history:

> Redemption does not come suddenly but appears as the logical and necessary function of Jewish history. Israel's labours of *tiqqun* are, *by definition, of a messianic character.* Final redemption is therefore no longer dissociated from the historical process that preceded it: "The redemption of Israel takes place by degrees."[128]

In this version the Messiah, far from bringing about restitution, is himself brought about by it—slowly, by degrees: "we shall have to build houses, dig wells, and plant vines and olive trees." Even in those forms of messianism which rely on human passivity, you have to be in anticipation, somehow ready and prepared, for the event to take place (it is never therefore wholly independent of man). And even the most scrupulous forms of gradualism, such as Kalischer's for example, have a latent utopian, not to say apocalyptic, streak: "And afterward the true Messiah will be revealed, together with all the promised beneficences; and the Evil Urge will be destroyed."[129]

On receiving the Balfour Declaration, which he had been so instrumental in producing—Ben-Gurion refers to him as the father of Balfour[130]—Weizmann comments: "Believe me, when I had the Balfour Declaration in my hand, I felt as if a sun ray had struck me; and I thought I heard the steps of the Messiah"—"But," he continues, "I remembered that the true Redeemer is said to come silently like a thief in the night."[131] For Weizmann, apparently blind to the messianic strand of his own discourse, what mattered was the slow, incremental labor of Zionism, its organic relation both to the soil and to itself. "To me," he writes in his memoir in words resonant of the Harbingers, "Zionism was something organic, which had to grow like a plant, had to be watched, watered and nursed, if it was to reach maturity."[132] In a thinly veiled criticism of Herzl, he insists, "I did not believe that things could be done in a hurry."[133] "In this slow and difficult struggle with the marshes and rocks of Palestine lies the greatest challenge to the creative forces of the Jewish people, its redemption from the abnormalities of exile."[134] Weizmann was fiercely secular: at the London Zionist Congress of 1900, he stated, "[I]f the rabbis are here as representatives of the synagogues that is anti-Jewish, for there are no synagogues in Judaism."[135] But while he seems to think he has relinquished a false messianic hope, in fact, like so many of the key players of Zionism, he has merely displaced it. "I lacked Herzl's wings," he wrote in 1927, "was able to achieve my task through hard and sorrowful work only."[136] "The doctrine of *tiqqun*," writes Scholem, "raised every Jew to the rank of protagonist in the great path of restitution."[137] In the words of Ben-Gurion, "Every man his own Messiah."[138]

In a famous letter to Franz Rosenzweig of 1926, Scholem wrote, "They think they have made Hebrew into a secular language, that they have removed its apocalyptic sting." But, he continues, every word "taken from the treasurehouse of well-worn terms is laden with explosives."[139] The explosives and apocalyptic sting are to be found in the common currency of everyday speech, in the vernacular of Israel's very self-definition. Expressions such as *memshalah u-mamlakhah* (rulership and kingdom), *yeshuah* (salvation), *tzur yisrael* (Rock of Israel), *aliya lakarka* (ascent to the land), *ge'ulah la-aretz* (redemption of the land), *hagshama* (literally "fulfillment" but denoting settlement of the frontiers). In the final lines of the 1948 Declaration of Independence, Diaspora Jewry is exhorted to "join forces with us in immigration and construction, to be at our right hand in the great endeavour to fulfil the age-old longing for the redemption of Israel." "We trust in the Rock of Israel."[140] At its most explosive, messianism sheds its religious colors and enters the language as violence: *bittahon*, which originally referred to trust in God, now denotes military security (for messianic Zionist Rabbi Zvi Tau, all wars against Israel are wars against the light of God).[141] Or Israel's early pioneering history is given cataclysmic dimension: *ha'apalah*, the term for prestate "illegal" immigration (immigration in defiance of Mandate quotas) originally meant a forbidden and catastrophic breakthrough. The language of secular Zionism bears the traces and scars of a messianic narrative that it barely seeks, or fails, to repress.

And there is something more. Israel famously made the "desert bloom." But even here, there is a chilling messianic streak. In Ezekiel, the End will be revealed when the mountains of Israel yield her produce, bear fruit; Rashi glosses: "When the land of Israel gives its fruit generously, the End is at hand."[142] Fruitfulness does not therefore just ward off disaster; it *ushers it in*. This at the very least is to make the land a supreme, and supremely ambivalent—Slavoj Žižek would call it *sublime*—object. After all, we tend to worship what we most fear. There are moments in the early writing when the encounter with the land inspires a kind of visionary terror or "horror religiosus," to use Kierkegaard's term. Arriving in Palestine in 1880, Eliezer Ben Yehuda proclaimed: "Yes! My feet brushed the Holy Land, the Land of the Fathers—and there was no joy in my heart, no thoughts, no inspiration, in my mind! It was as if my brain was empty or frozen, prey to terror. The only thing, the only feeling that filled me was that of overwhelming fear."[143] In his memoir, Ben-Gurion cites a letter from Yehuda to Rashi Fein: "[O]nly upon this soil, soaked with the blood of thousands of our finest sons, can our nation exist."[144] The land is sacred because it is stained; when it is most fruitful, the end is nigh. In this these early Zionists come perilously close to their most radical, vitriolic opponents, for whom Zionism's foothold in the Holy Land was a demonstration of the vileness that had always inhered in it. For Rebbe Shapira, spokesperson for the radical ultra-Orthodox wing of Hungarian Jewry in the 1920s and virulent anti-Zionist, the adversary has chosen his dwelling in Jerusalem; Palestine is at once holy and defiled.

The more I have read of this writing, the more convinced I found myself becoming that the classic and famous Zionist claim—Palestine was a land without a people—was not just a blatant lie but a cover. The draw of Palestine resided at least partly in fear. Yehuda's comment suggests that if there was a void, it was one that opened, as he lighted on the soil, in order to fill his mind with terror. Not for nothing does Scholem warn of the "*blazing* landscape of redemption."[145] My settlers in Allon Shvut ended our interview by asking us to admire the views—"breathtaking—absolutely" "tremendous"—as we drove off, barely moments after telling us how scared they were (we had had to drive along the settler road, on which no Palestinian is allowed to travel, in a bullet-proof car). "Blood and fire cover the country," Uri Avnery writes in his dispatch for *Gush-Shalom* of June 14, 2003, entitled "Children of Death," the clearest sign for him that the objective of Sharon—to wreck any viable future—is being achieved: "In our days, historians wonder what folly took possession of the Jewish people 1,930 years ago, causing them to start a hopeless rebellion against the Roman empire and bringing utter destruction upon the Jewish commonwealth in Palestine. A hundred years from now, historians will ask themselves what folly took possession of this people, causing it to elect Sharon, a bloody person who has not done anything in life apart from shedding blood."[146] "When you have sunk to the lowest level," God says to Israel, "I will redeem you."

There is of course another more obvious sense in which Zionism can be seen as a secular version of Redemption. Because faith, belief in Orthodoxy, was declining throughout the age of Enlightenment, the nation became the new God (Scholem shares with Arendt the belief that Shabtaism was the catastrophic rupture that made this later secularization possible). Paradoxically it is the failure of Orthodox Judaism that allows Zionism, and the land, to swell under the pressure of messianic zeal. No one illustrates this journey, I think, more clearly than David Ben-Gurion, bit player in this first chapter but crucial to the story to come. A secular Jew, like so many of the key figures in the early political history of Zionism, Ben-Gurion bequeathed to Israel in his rhetoric the messianic destiny of the nation-in-waiting.

"Without a messianic, emotional, ideological impulse, without the vision of restoration and redemption," he states in his memoir, "there is no earthly reason why even oppressed and underprivileged Jews . . . should wander off to Israel of all places. . . . The immigrants were seized with an immortal vision of redemption which became the principal motivation of their lives."[147] Without messianism, no nation. For Ben-Gurion the greatest threat to Diaspora Jewry was assimilation (he described the dispersion as "shocking'); messianism was the answer to a prayer: "The emancipation of the Jews led not to assimilation but to a new expression of their national uniqueness and Messianic longing."[148] Compare Kook: "The anticipation of redemption is the force which keeps exilic Judaism alive, and the Judaism of the land of Israel is salvation itself."[149] Ben-Gurion is talking about the survival not of Judaism but of the Jews. Now the Bible is set the task of legitimating Jewish peoplehood. As Judaism transmutes into national identity, it lifts with it the inspiration of the faith. Like Weizmann, Ben-Gurion acknowledges Zionism as a magnificent violation of the reality of the world. Given the unreason of the project—"there is *no earthly reason*"—only messianism would do.

Ben-Gurion came to Palestine from Poland in 1906, three years after the Kishinev pogrom and the year after the aborted revolution in Russia of 1905. He therefore inherited the mantle of what Hertzberg terms the "neo-messianic" fervor of the Eastern European Jews. These were the "children of an aborted modernity" whose added urgency, and revolutionary zeal, were at least partly borne on the wings of despair; they could not share with their Central European counterparts the confidence that Zionism was the last stumbling block in the inevitable march of enlightenment and liberalism across the globe. Hertzberg describes Ben-Gurion as "their greatest survivor." "What made it possible," he asks, "for the 'neo-messianists' vehemently to deny God and yet insist that they could rebuild the Jewish nation only on the land He had promised to Abraham?"[150]

It is worth noting the extent to which the language of salvation and redemption saturates Ben-Gurion's prose. "The return to Zion and to the Bible is a supreme expression of the rebirth and resurgence of the Jewish people," he proclaimed in an address delivered in Jerusalem in 1950, two years after the creation of Israel, "and the more complete the return the nearer we will come to full political and spiritual salvation."[151] Note the equation between the political and the spiritual; in both spheres salvation must be "full." Ben-Gurion's socialist Zionism—no class of Jew will be excluded—makes sense only in the context of this total and totalizing vision: "Socialist Zionism is Zionism not content with the redemption of part of the people, but strives for the redemption of the whole people, and for *a complete and absolute redemption of the people.*"[152] Note, too, how his language slides from inclusiveness to totality to the absolute. "The thing we call Zionism and the thing we call Socialism came into being *only in order to realise our will.*"[153] Secular messianism—"complete and absolute redemption"—usurps the will of God on behalf of the nation. "The Bible is our Mandate."[154]

For Ben-Gurion the essential determining events of Jewish history would remain throughout his life the Exodus, Mount Sinai, the conquest of the land by Joshua, and finally the founding of the State of Israel. Under pressure of the biblical narrative, two thousand years of history fall into the dust. At the same time, a form of statism laced with messianic fervor usurps the socialist vision of his earliest days—the working nation (encapsulated in the early Labor formula *Am Oved*) is replaced by *mamlakhtiyut*, a statist nation grounded on messianic vision (the word combines statehood and kingdom).[155] It is a characteristic of "messianism in power," writes Zionist historian Shlomo Avineri in an essay on the "post-Ben-Gurion ethic" that he subtitles "The Nemesis of Messianism," that it ceases to yearn for new moral horizons and becomes pure defense of the authority of the state.[156] Slowly but surely, the universalism of the socialist dream is absorbed back into the particularity of Jewish destiny:

"Ours is a messianic movement, and that is the most suitable word, for it is a specifically Jewish expression."[157]

As if Zionist Labor had sprung full-formed out of the Jewish prophetic tradition—a tradition Ben-Gurion was not shy in invoking (in 1959, he is described as sounding like an "agnostic prophet," a cross "between Isaiah and the hero of *Invictus*").[158] "I am one who believes in the prophecy of Isaiah. 'I will bring thy seed from the East and gather thee from the West; I will say to the North: "Give up" and to the South: "Keep not back, bring My sons from afar, and my daughters from the end of the Earth".' "[159] As we will see, this Jewish exclusivity would have major implications for the future of the state. But we can already notice how it violates one of the professed aims of the Zionist movement—that Israel should take its place alongside the other nations of the world, that it should become normal, "like unto the nations."

After the founding of the state, Ben-Gurion's exhortations take on one repeated form, the call to the ingathering of the exiles. For Scholem, such a call is in itself apocalyptic—the End had begun; only the call to ingathering was still required.[160] In Lurianic Kabbalah, ingathering refers to the redemption of the divine sparks that have fallen into the *qelippoth*, or evil of the world. Once again, this mystical doctrine translates directly into political reality on the ground. Nathan Shapira, who had come from Cracow to Palestine, based his writing on Lurianic doctrine. Ten years before the outbreak of Shabtaism, he had this to say in his work, *The Goodness of the Land*, on the eschatological relations between Palestinian and Diaspora Jews:

> Those of the Diaspora who endeavoured to come to Palestine to receive a pure soul, who spared neither money nor efforts and came by sea and land and were not afraid of being drowned in the sea or captured by cruel masters; because they were concerned primarily for their spirits and their souls and not for their bodies and money, therefore they were turned into spirits—measure for measure.[161]

Words, Scholem wryly observes, resonant of the differences between "Zionists" and "men of the dispersion': "to use contemporary conceptions that come to mind."[162] Even for the Orthodox who denounced Zionism, the sole meaning of the coming of the Messiah was "[t]o gather in the exiled of Israel."[163] To this day, Israel has not shed its sense of divinely appointed superiority over Diaspora Jews.

At moments in Ben-Gurion's language, ingathering appears as the ultimate goal, not just the means to the creation of the state but its most fundamental raison d'être: "The promotion of Jewish immigration is not only a central task of the Jewish State—but the essential justification for its establishment and existence."[164]

We know of course what "ingathering" means. "We must create a Jewish majority in the Land of Israel in the next twenty years."[165] "There can be no stable and strong Jewish state so long as it has a Jewish majority of only 60 per cent."[166] In 1931, Weizmann was forced to resign from the presidency of the Zionist Congress after giving an interview to the Jewish Telegraphic Agency in which he said there was no need for a Jewish majority in the Land of Israel: "I have no understanding of and no sympathy for the demand for a Jewish majority in

Palestine. Majority does not guarantee security, majority is not necessary for the development of Jewish civilisation and culture. The world will construe this demand only in the sense that we want to drive out the Arabs."[167] This is the crux for the critics of political Zionism who will be the focus of the next chapter. In fact Weizmann had been one of the strongest advocates of transfer of the Arabs as a way of securing the Jewish identity of the state. Ingathering and expulsion are two sides of the same coin—only the Jews must increase. "The Zionist enterprise so far . . . has been fine and good in its own time, and could do with 'land-buying,' " wrote Joseph Weitz, director of the Jewish National Land Fund from 1932, in a diary entry of December 19, 1940, "but this will not bring about the State of Israel; that must come all at once, in the manner of a Salvation (this is the secret of the Messianic idea); and there is no way without transferring the Arabs from here to the neighbouring countries, to transfer them all."[168] Transfer—a concept spoken openly again in Israel today—reveals itself here unapologetically as a form of salvation. Nor is there any naïveté whatsoever in these views: "From the point of view of mankind's humanistic morality, we were in the wrong in [taking the land] from the Canaanites," states Rabbi Shlomo Aviner of Gush Emunim. "There is only one catch. The command of God ordered us to be the people of the land of Israel."[169] "Let them go to the Arab countries," says Chana Bart of Kfar Darom.[170]

"*We must*," Ben-Gurion responds to Weizmann in 1931, "*double our numbers*."[171] And beyond: "Our State will survive and fulfill its historic vision if the Jewish people and its government will succeed in attracting and absorbing immigration *on an ever increasing scale*."[172] Increase also harbors a eugenic task for the burgeoning nation-state: "Any Jewish woman who, as far as it depends on her, does not bring into the world at least four healthy children is shirking her [sacred] duty to the nation" (he famously offered one hundred lirot to any woman on the birth of her tenth child).[173] None of this has gone away. In August 2003, to a huge international outcry, the Knesset passed a new law preventing Palestinians who marry Israelis from living in Israel; Palestinian-Israeli couples will be forced to leave or live apart, but anyone other than a Palestinian who marries an Israeli will be entitled to Israeli citizenship. July 2004 saw an extension of the temporary order prohibiting Arab citizens from marrying Palestinians from the territories unless they emigrate. The parliament also passed, on preliminary reading, a law that will stop relatives of non-Jewish, naturalized Israeli citizens from uniting with their families.[174] In 2002 a delegation of rabbis traveled to Lima to convert a group of South American Indians to Judaism on condition that they come and live in Israel (on arrival they were bused immediately to the settlements).[175]

Speaking of the plan to construct a new neighborhood south of Jerusalem, half of which will fall outside the 1967 Green Line, deputy mayor Yehoshua Polak—who holds the municipal planning and construction brief—commented in June 2004, "We want as many Jews as possible in Jerusalem, to influence the demographic situation."[176] It is one of the ironies of this story that demographic fear is today pushing many Israelis toward a two-state solution—if Israel holds on to the territories, by 2020 Jews will be outnumbered by Arabs. In March Sharon announced his plan to attract one million Jews to Israel over the next five years. In this dispensation, the Jew has become the messianic fulfillment of himself.

In a famous article, the psychoanalyst W. R. Bion tried to account for the psychopathology of groups.[177] All groups, he insisted, have inside them a "work group" that consists of the concrete, realizable aspirations held by the group in common. But no group is ever free of what he referred to as the "basic assumption," of which he names three: the leadership group (the leader is wholly answerable for the fate of the group), the fight-flight group (the group exists in order to fight or to flee), and the pairing group (the group is sustained by an invisible couple at its core). All three contain a redemptive streak—be it an absolute faith in the leader, a fear of attack as the defining, saving, feature of the group, or the hopeful expectation that group therapy, with an ideal pair at its core, can revolutionize the world (in each case the faith, fear, or hope is deluded). Participation in such assumptions, he writes, "requires no training, experience, or mental development." It is "instantaneous, inevitable and instinctive."[178]

Bion was attempting to push Freud's account of group psychology beyond Freud. Beyond neurosis to psychosis. Beyond repression to delusion. The phenomenon he is describing exceeds the classic psychoanalytic account in being, as he puts it, "far more bizarre": "I know of no experience that demonstrates more clearly than the group experience," he writes, "the dread with which a questioning attitude is regarded."[179]

Bion's distinction between the work group and the basic assumption group can, I think, help us here, as indeed can his point that when a basic assumption is in play, questioning—critique, dissent—becomes, not just impermissible, but an object of "dread." For Bion, fear of dissent—we might note this in relation to Israel and more widely post-9/11—would be the clearest sign of being unconsciously driven, of fleeing one part of your own mind. If only you would let yourself know, you are having an internal argument with yourself. In the chapter that follows, I will be suggesting that Zionism had this kind of self-knowledge, which has subsequently been lost. Of course no one would disagree that the early settlers in Israel came with a work ethic that they proceeded in many ways to realize. Even the most fervent critics of political Zionism, such as Arendt would praise the Jewish "upbuilding" of Palestine. But this actuality, the materialization of Israel's vision of itself, is laced with the spirit of messianic fulfillment. And this in turn serves to fuel, justify, redeem state violence in the throes of denying itself. The so-called division or split between messianic and secular Zionism conceals a latent affiliation of powerful and often deadly ramification and scope. To put the argument of this first chapter in Bion's terms, a messianic basic assumption group veils itself behind work. Nothing, we might say, works as hard as redemption.

I have tried here to trace the line that runs from messianism to the heart of Zionism, including secular Zionism—that is, to the heart of Zionism *even when, or perhaps especially when, it does not know it is there.* We cannot therefore relegate messianism to the religious Zionists and Orthodox anti-Zionists, any more than we can to Gush Emunim or indeed the even more fervently fundamentalist and ruthlessly messianic movement of Kach. We are talking of the "*slow but steady*" penetration of the civic culture by a vision that many of Israel's citizens do not explicitly embrace (for the most powerful studies of the place of fundamentalism inside Israel, we should turn to the writings of human rights activist and Holocaust survivor Israel Shahak).[180] We are talking about the power of fervor, not only to trample over the rights of its opponents, but to trump the reason of the group mind. Messianism, as unconscious inspiration, is in the air and soil of Israel. However bad things get—perhaps the worse things get—daily it translates itself into the earth. It lends fire to an ingathering that, it is fervently hoped in the dreams of the nation, will never cease.

What I have been describing can perhaps be best read as a problem stemming from the inner conflict that Israel has always had with itself. The more the nation tried to normalize itself, the more it sought to rest its claim to the land on the labor and presence of the Jewish people, so it weakened its case against the rights of the indigenous peoples of Palestine who were making their case on identical grounds (hence the urgent insistence that only Jewish labor redeems). Only a higher court could therefore arbitrate. If not destiny, then by what right? For the second generation of native-born Israelis, this dilemma is the peculiar consequence of secular Zionism's success: "Precisely because those born there no longer saw their country as a land of destiny," comments Eliezer Schweid at the end of his study, "their right to have it as a homeland appeared more and more in doubt."[181] If messianism keeps returning, and will not relinquish its hold on the psyche of the nation, it might paradoxically be because it is the answer to a secular prayer. And if apocalyptic messianism remains so resonant, might it not also be because it is the only way of acknowledging, if only indirectly, the violence and unreason—"there is no earthly reason"—of the claim?

To return, one more time, to Scholem. In calling up Shabtai Zvi from the mists of time, he entrusted to himself the role of archaeologist of Zionism's forgotten prehistory. But while he certainly believed that Zvi's movement was the central liberating event in modern Jewish history and that it accounted for much of the hidden creativity of the Jewish tradition, he also knew that what he was reviving was demonic. Not for nothing did he devote his work to this strange fervent figure when he was living in the Holy City, while the clouds of a new Jewish future, heralded as a new messianic dawn, were gathering overhead. As early as 1928, he expressed his fears of the link between Shabtaism and Zionism: "The messianic phraseology of Zionism, especially in its decisive moments, is not the least of those Sabbatian temptations which could bring disaster to the renewal of Judaism."[182]

Scholem was active in Brit Shalom, which had called for a limit to immigration. "I do not believe," he wrote in 1931 to Walter Benjamin from Jerusalem, where Benjamin would not follow him, "that there is such a thing as 'solution to the Jewish Question' in the sense of a normalisation of the Jews, and I certainly do not think this question can be solved in Palestine."[183] In 1929, following the Arab riots at the Wailing Wall, Scholem had refused to make books from his private library available to the Jewish committee preparing its case for the British investigating commission. Doubtless the committee hoped that the books of this revered scholar of Jewish history and thought—now established in his chair of Jewish mysticism at the Hebrew University of Jerusalem, which had opened in 1925—would establish a prior, or higher, spiritual claim to the Wall. For Scholem this was a matter for political negotiation with the Arabs; possession of the land should not be grounded in a religious claim. For this refusal he was roundly denounced as an anti-Zionist. In the same year, in his dispute with Yehudah Burla in the pages of *Davar*, he stated: "I absolutely deny that Zionism is a messianic movement and that it has the right to employ religious terminology for political goals. The redemption of the Jewish people, which as a Zionist I desire, is in no way identical with the religious redemption I hope for in the future" (complete redemption he condemned as "imperialist").[184] Scholem was, that is to say, a true believer in messianism on condition that it not be conflated with the political actualization of a religious dream. The extent of his own personal disillusionment can be gleaned from these lines taken from "Encounter with Zion and the World," which he composed on June 29, 1930:

> What was within is now without,
> The dream twists into violence,
> And once again we stand outside,
> And Zion is without form or sense.[185]

In his book *A Place among the Nations*, Benjamin Netanyahu cites, with unqualified admiration, Vladimir (Ze'ev) Jabotinsky's warning of the imminent catastrophe for European Jewry delivered in Warsaw in 1938, not just for its prescience—"catastrophe is nigh . . . I see a horrible vision"—but for foretelling the "rebirth" of the Jewish State: "I want to say something else to you on this day, the ninth of Av," Jabotinsky began his speech, the day commemorating the destruction of the First and Second Temples and reputedly the day on which Shabtai Zvi was born.[186] Vladimir Jabotinsky, founder of Revisionist Zionism, was the specific target of Scholem's critique of messianism, inspiration for Netanyahu and many of today's Israeli Right who are ruling the country. Unapologetically, he ushered back into the nation's discourse Zionism's apocalyptic strain.[187] "Few," comments Netanyahu, "could see the catastrophe coming, and fewer still could share in Jabotinsky's note of hope."[188] Echoing the apocalyptic tone, all too willing to sweep up both the catastrophe and regeneration of his people, Netanyahu adds, "The Jewish people was approaching the end."[189]

In his 1971 essay "Toward an Understanding of the Messianic Idea in Judaism," Scholem asks, "Can Jewish history manage to re-enter concrete reality without being destroyed by the messianic claim which [that re-entry] is bound to bring up from its depths?"[190] For Scholem, messianic political Zionism was in danger of "triumphing itself to death."[191] It has been the purpose of this first chapter to suggest that his warning went unheard.

Chapter 2

"Imponderables in thin air": Zionism as Psychoanalysis (Critique)

There is nothing so barbarous, so evil, that the human mind cannot foster it, given suitable conditions.

—Ahad Ha'am, "Ancestor Worship" (1897)

In Eretz Israel, a Jew does not need to feel his national pulse beating every hour; in this sense, he is completely healthy.

—A. D. Gordon to Ahad Ha'am (1912)

The Israeli army's Chief of Staff, Lieutenant-General Moshe Yaalon . . . told some of his soldiers that he did not care if the military "looks like lunatics".

—Chris McGreal, " 'The Real Obstacle to Peace Is Not Terror, but Sabotage by Sharon-Backed Army' " (June 20, 2003)

The hero of Theodor Herzl's 1902 novel *Altneuland*, Dr. Friedrich Loewenberg, is a suicidal depressive.[1] Trained as a lawyer, disaffected from his profession and society, he answers an advertisement: "Wanted, cultured and despairing young man willing to try last experiment with his life. Write N.O.Body c/o this."[2] The project—the plan of a Gentile Mr. Kingscourt—is to forsake human society and go to live on a Pacific island, a rock on Cook's Archipelago, with two servants: a "dumb Negro" and a native from Tahiti "pulled from the sea when trying to put an end to his life."[3] "There was one last experiment left," Kingscourt explains to Friedrich, "absolute loneliness, a great unheard-of loneliness. No more truck with humanity, with its miserable fights, its dirty treacheries. The true, the profound solitude, without desire and without effort. . . . This solitude is the paradise humanity has lost through its own fault."[4]

On the way they pass by Palestine, and almost as an afterthought, Kingscourt suggests to his companion that they visit. " 'Wouldn't you like to pay a visit to your homeland?' 'What do you mean, do you want to return to Trieste?' 'Not at all,' roared Kingscourt. 'Your homeland is in front of you, not behind. Palestine!' " To which Friedrich replies: "You're under a misapprehension. I've not the slightest connection with Palestine. I've never been there."[5] The visit is wretched. Friedrich is plunged into another bout of depression—part orientalist revulsion (Jaffa is full of "motley oriental misery"), part disaffection with his own people. "However deeply I probe into my racial subconscious," Friedrich comments after a visit to the Wailing Wall in Jerusalem, "I still fail to find anything that I have in common with these degenerate exploiters of our national mourning."[6]

After a twenty-year sojourn on their deserted island, they return—again at Kingscourt's suggestion, Friedrich reluctantly—to find a flourishing country, a Jewish homeland that is yet cosmopolitan, multiethnic, and multifaith: "You will find besides our own synagogues, churches and mosques—and even Buddhist and Brahmin temples."[7] Run by the New Society on the model of co-operatives, this Palestine promotes something close to Tony Blair's "Third Way": "With us the individual is neither ground small between the millstones of capitalism, nor beheaded by the levelling-down process of socialism."[8] As an entirely new civilization, the country has been able to import the accumulated experience and technology of all the advanced nations of the world. There is no state, no ownership of land; nobody has legal title to the holy sites of Jerusalem, which are governed under the principle of "*res sacrae extra commercium*," the only way to guarantee they will remain the "common property of all believers forever."[9]

Altneuland is a remarkable document of the Zionist imagination but not quite for the reasons for which it is best known: as Herzl's fictional actualization of a dream he would not himself see fulfilled. It was written by Herzl at a time when he was dispirited by his lack of progress toward Jewish statehood. Negotiations with the sultan to open his empire to Jewish refugees—the "Turkish imbroglio," as it became known—had just failed, and he had turned to the cooperative vision of Berliner Franz Oppenheimer, who had written a series of articles on collective labor in *Die Welt* (Oppenheimer had taken his ideas from Nahman Syrkin, alongside A. D. Gordon another founding father of socialist Zionism). The novel is often dismissed. It was severely criticized at the time for its lack of Jewish national content. Its cosmopolitanism gave particular offense. In fact the novel contains as much pure colonialist fantasy as surprisingly progressive thought. When I interviewed Yossi Beilin in 2002, he answered a question I put to him, about Zionist blindness toward the Arabs, by citing an encounter in the novel with a Muslim doctor of chemistry, Rashid Bey—who studied in Berlin and speaks German—whose father Herzl portrays as "one of those who immediately grasped that Jewish immigration could only be beneficial to all, and he profited from our economic boom."[10] It was one of the most strongly held beliefs of early Zionists that Jewish settlement in Palestine, regardless of the dispossession, would be to the benefit of Jews and Arabs alike. This in itself would provide a cure for anti-Semitism—impoverished Jewish migrants (Herzl always insisted the poor would be the first to go) would, in a miraculous transformation, become the patrons of the East. "The Jews have brought us wealth and health. Why should we harbour evil thoughts about them?"[11] "We are not stupid people," Beilin glossed the Arab doctor without a trace of self-consciousness, "we can learn, we can be like yourself"; Bey is "very happy" that the "Jewish state exists."[12]

In fact there is no state. In this, Herzl is being consistent: "And you want to found a state there?" Hohenlohe, representative of Frederic, Grand Duke of Baden, asked Herzl, on the eve of his 1898 meeting with the kaiser, to which, according to his diary record, Herzl replied, "We want autonomy and self-defense."[13] And if there is no hostility between national groups, it is because there is also no ethnically or religiously defined identity—there is in a way no nation. "Neither I nor my friends," David Litwak, future president of the Jewish Society, explains to Kingscourt, "make the slightest distinction between one man and another. We don't ask about anyone's race or religion. It's enough for us that he is human." You can read this as denial—Herzl, and not only Herzl, famously refusing to acknowledge the violent force of Zionism's own nationalism and the Arab nationalism it would provoke ("we must expropriate gently . . . we shall try to spirit the penniless population across the border," Herzl wrote in his diary in 1895, two years before *Der Judenstaat*).[14] On the other hand, *Altneuland*—open, secular, pluralist—also reads at times like a post-Zionist dream. There are moments that could almost have been lifted out of *The Dignity of Difference*, by chief rabbi of Great Britain Jonathan Sacks—before the cuts Sacks made when the Orthodox world's top rabbinic authority, Rabbi Yosef Shalom Elyashiv of Jerusalem, ruled some of his statements heretical and the book unfit to be brought into any home.[15] In *Altneuland*, Friedrich is watching a Muslim at prayer: "He prays in another house to the same God who is above us all. But the houses of prayer are close to one another, and I think the prayers mingle somewhere and go up together to our Father."[16] The rabbi ruled it heretical to assert that God could speak in more than one voice.

Even more crucial for the purposes of this discussion, the "upbuilding" of the country is something that the main protagonist, and therefore the reader, never sees:

"It is the transition I miss" (remember they are gone for twenty years). "I can *not*," Friedrich bemoans, "grasp how it came about with my reason."[17] Beyond reason, Herzl makes the creation of Israel something unrepresentable, which the human brain cannot grasp and the eyes cannot see. There is always a risk with utopia that it might not quite believe in itself. Most of the novel after Friedrich's return depicts the efforts of those living in the country to make him accept its new reality (also a crude narrative device so that everything can be patiently explained, a bit like the ghastly first scene of *The Tempest*). The fact is that the protagonist of *Altneuland*, whose journey is our journey as readers, is a disaffected, non-Jewish Jew, as we might say. Depressed, suicidal, missing—to the creation of the new homeland and to himself. There is of course a simple reading: a dispirited young German Jew of Central Europe is redeemed by the rebirth of Palestine. But I believe Herzl is also offering an unintentional diagnosis of Zionism. Running under the euphoria—the vision and messianic elation of the first chapter—there is something not quite right (there was also, as we have seen, something not quite right inside that vision). The birth of a nation might be cause for celebration; it might be cure. But written across the heart of the narrative, as something it cannot quite forget, is a counsel of despair.

Theodor Herzl was a depressive. He was also, as his biographer Amos Elon observes, the most prodigious diary keeper, which means that the man most often credited with the creation of organized Zionism, who devoted his life—largely unsuccessfully—to international diplomacy to that end, leaves a double legacy:

of realpolitik and a window to the soul. "Few men of action," Elon writes in the introduction, "have left such a wealth of unconscious indices to their neuroses."[18] In a diary entry of 1879—he was nineteen—he writes: "I have much cause to complain about the changes in my moods, to exalt to high heaven, to be deadly depressed, soon to delude myself with hope . . . then again to die but soon to be rejected by death. . . . Pain is the basic feeling of life."[19] Herzl shares these states of exaltation and depression with Shabtai Zvi who, as Scholem stressed, also veered between dejection and manic illumination (quoting Isaiah—"I will ascend above the heights of the clouds"—he felt himself literally floating on air).[20] By his own account, Herzl wrote *Der Judenstaat* in a state of mental intoxication. He felt he was losing his mind: "It has possessed me beyond the limits of consciousness."[21] To a man who encountered him in the street during its composition, he apparently looked like someone suffering a psychotic shock or risen from a terrible disease.[22] Herzl wrote the pamphlet "walking, standing, lying down; in the street, at table, in the dead of night when I was driven from sleep. . . . The whole idea now absorbs me to such an extent that I relate everything to it, as a lover to his beloved."[23] Whenever he lost confidence in notions he himself describes as "ludicrous, exaggerated, crazy," he would listen to Wagner.[24] It was only when Wagner was not playing at the Paris opera that he had any doubts as to the truth of his ideas. (According to one story it was the same Paris performance of Wagner, when—without knowledge or foreknowledge of each other—they were both present on the same evening, that inspired Herzl to write *Der Judenstaat*, and Hitler *Mein Kampf*.)

The depression of Zionism is not, however, confined to the creative mania of Herzl alone. In January 1902, Weizmann wrote to Leo Motzkin: "[My health] is not good. As a matter of fact I went to see the doctor yesterday. He diagnosed neurasthenia and weakness of the respiratory organs. *Uebermüdung und Ueberreizung* (overfatigue and overexcitement)."[25] Disillusioned with Herzl, feeling the cause flounder, he had written to his fiancée the previous year, "We are nervous, unstrung, flabby, unfit for the Jewish cause." "Our sensitiveness has made us vacillating creatures."[26] It is too easy to read these comments as Jewish self-hatred, a recycling of anti-Semitic stereotypes—of which Zionism and Herzl in particular, it must be stressed, were far from free. Rather they seem to me to testify to a form of recognition. Too much was being demanded (excitement, or overstimulation, wears the spirit thin). In order for this dream to be brought to fruition, too much—violently—would have to be performed. "The captain weeps," writes Weizmann to his fiancée in the same letter; "The man setting out to war weeps." For Ilan Pappe, one of the key new historians who have been rewriting the history of Israel over the past decade, these tropes would reveal themselves as the first signs of Zionism's delusory language—"purity of arms," "shoot and weep"—which he has done so much to lay bare. But in this early stage, I also see them as a reluctant acknowledgment. Zionism would ask *too much*. To achieve the dream of Zion, you would have to place yourself in a psychically unoccupiable place—high or low, exalted or in despair. Zionism could be forged only in a state "beyond consciousness" (as in *Altneuland*, the making of the nation cannot be grasped by the conscious mind).

For Herzl, there was an even more personal and tragic price—two of his three children, Pauline and Hans, would commit suicide; the third, Trude, was committed to a mental institution after the birth of her son, Stephan Theodor; she survived but then died in Theresienstadt, while her son, who was saved by being sent to England, killed himself in Washington in 1945 a few months after being hailed as Herzl's descendant in a triumphant visit to Palestine.[27] Zionism—this was the consistent reproach of Herzl's wife, Julie Naschauser—demands too much.

"A sentiment which I believed I had suppressed beyond recall," Moses Hess says of his awakening to the idea of nationality, "is alive again."[28] As if a political movement could be drawn, almost unmediated, out of the unconscious. What distinguished Zionist socialism from democratic socialism, writes Georges Bensoussan, was an idea of the nation based on "land, descent and the dead," whereas European socialism was loath to allow the "collective unconscious" into its midst.[29] "I have read your *Judenstaat* twice," Nordau wrote to Herzl in February 1896. "It was particular courage to have admitted to feelings that other Jews had pushed back into the depths of their unconscious."[30] Hannah Arendt described him as "in touch with the subterranean currents of history" (less generously as a "crackpot").[31] "We must prepare," writes Leon Pinsker in his 1882 *AutoEmancipation!*, another key pre-Herzlian Zionist text, "for a great outcry. The stirrings of this struggle will doubtless be ascribed by most of the Jews who have, with reason, become timorous and sceptical, to the unconscious convulsions of an organism dangerously ill."[32] Only the "madmen of the spirit," A. D. Gordon writes in 1921, will be equal to the task ahead.[33]

Herzl's *Altneuland* was published two years after Freud's *The Interpretation of Dreams*. Zionism and psychoanalysis are companions of the spirit, their journey coterminous even if radically divergent as to their ends. Precisely because Zionism had to make itself out of nothing—create a unity, a language, a homeland where there was none before—it knows itself as a child of the psyche, a dream, a figment of the brain. Herzl was after all a playwright before anything else (the first, and until Vaclav Havel, the only political figure known to have such a beginning). The unconscious, wrote Freud in one of his most famous definitions, is "ein andere Schauplatz," another scene.[34] Herzl's projects for the creation of a Jewish state all crumbled on their own diplomatically fueled grandeur (kaiser, sultan, one imbroglio after another). But Herzl may also, in his magisterial failure, have been wise to something. Like the unconscious, Zionism had to be staged (as only a playwright might understand). Zionism was a conjuring act. "They escaped to Palestine," Hannah Arendt wrote of the early Zionists, "as one might wish to escape to the moon."[35] Zionism always involved a form of "insubordination" against reality and the demands of reason. "The politics of peoples," declared Arthur Ruppin in 1936, resigning from the organization Brit Shalom, which struggled to preserve relations with the Arabs, "are not determined by rational considerations but by their instinctive drives."[36]

As if to say, he who enters here plumbs the depths of the political mind. This makes Zionism, for better and worse, the most wonderful exemplar of the work of the psyche in the constitution of the modern nation-state. Ruppin continues: "All the economic advantages and rational considerations will not lead the Arabs to relinquish sovereignty over Palestine in favour of the Jews, since, in their eyes, it belongs to them."[37] Reason will not settle it. You cannot have an argument with a dream. "Men are ruled by the simple and the fantastic," Herzl states in conversation with the Bavarian nobleman Baron Maurice de Hirsch. "It is astonishing . . . with what little intelligence the world is ruled."[38] "Believe me," he continues to Hirsch in a subsequent letter, "the politics of an entire people—especially one that is scattered all over the world—can only be made out of *imponderables that float high in the thin air.*"[39]

If Zionism knows its own unconscious dimension, there are, however, two very different ways in which such an acknowledgment can take shape. Herzl's way is the more obvious: " 'A flag? What's that? A stick with a cloth rag?' No, a flag, sir, is more than that. . . . It is indeed the only thing for which [men] are willing to die in masses, provided one educates them for it."[40] To call this protofascist is simply to recognize how miraculously efficient fascism is in such training of bodies and minds: "men are ready to die in masses if you train them for it." In a democracy, on the other hand, as we have seen in the aftermath of the Iraq war, while you may have no control over military decisions, you are at least allowed to ask, if only after the fact, why on earth you went to war. Today in Israel, refuseniks unwilling to serve in the occupied territories are being sent to jail (in fact U.S. troops publicly expressing dismay at extended service in Iraq have faced disciplinary measures).

The nation "dreads" dissent. Against the dominant rhetoric that legitimate fear justifies such dread, I would argue that it is because Israel silences dissent that it has most to fear. But there is another strand to Zionism to be found in writers like Martin Buber, Arendt, Hans Kohn, and Ahad Ha'am that provides the profoundest analysis of these dangers, dangers which—it is my argument in this chapter—have to be understood as much in psychic as in political terms. These dissenters were articulate, vocal, throughout the crucial period leading up to the formation of the nation, although inside Israel their voices have been mostly silenced since. Arendt's ideas, writes Amnon Raz-Krakotzkin, "became irrelevant when what she foresaw came to be real"; they were deemed "unrealistic" in proportion as "reality" proved her correct.[41] National passion, as we have already seen, defies reality, since reality is rarely the yardstick of the group. It is for me therefore one of the strengths of Zionism—one of the reasons why it should not be dismissed, even or especially by its critics—that it could have produced this dissenting analysis from within. Like Scholem, all these writers witnessed in their lifetime the triumph of the Jewish nation that none of them could have confidently predicted, but the shape it assumed before their eyes made this a cause less for elation than for lament. This did not stop them from espousing the Jewish cause, nor indeed from advocating a Jewish home in Palestine. But they each believed that Zionism could have taken a different path from the one it proclaimed, and still proclaims, as its destiny. All of them except Arendt took up residence in Palestine. Imagine how hard it must have been to pull against the drift, to have been anything other than euphoric in 1948. Today theirs is the still resonant, melancholic, counternarrative to the birth of a nation-state.

At the heart of Zionism, writes Martin Buber in his article "Zionism and 'Zionism,' " published on May 27, 1948, two weeks after the establishment of Israel, there is an "internal contradiction that reaches to the depths of human existence."[42] Two notions of national rebirth. Both require a return to Palestine. But whereas one desires to become a "normal" nation with "a land, a language and independence," the other, outside political time, aims to restore the spirit: "the spirit would build the life, like a dwelling, or like flesh."[43] These two tendencies, which have been "running about next to each other from ancient times," represent the division between the task of truth and justice, and the wish—"all too natural"—to be like other nations.[44] Like Arendt, Buber takes Zionism to task for being the real form of assimilation. "The Zionists were the only ones who sincerely wanted assimilation," writes Arendt, "namely, 'normalisation' of the people ('to be a people like all other peoples')."[45] "Of all the many kinds of assimilation in the course of our history," Buber had written in 1939, "this nationalist assimilation is the most terrifying, the most dangerous."[46] The ancient Hebrews did not succeed in becoming a normal nation: "Today," he writes in 1948, "the Jews are succeeding at it to a terrifying degree."[47] Zionism should not have created, or tried to create, a normal nation.

Buber's distinction between the spirit building the life and the normality of nations is therefore mapped onto a distinction between truth and justice, on the one hand, and terror or fear: "today the Jews are succeeding to a terrifying degree" (that a nation's triumph, as much as external threat, can be a cause for fear is not something we hear in Israel today). "Where," he asks, "do truth and justice determine our deeds?"[48] Most simply, crucially, Buber is objecting to the injustice being perpetrated against the Arabs: "what nation will allow itself to be demoted from the position of majority to that of minority without a fight?"[49] But Buber's argument contains a complex psychic dimension. His question "Where do truth and justice determine our deeds . . ." in fact continues "either inwardly or outwardly?" "I said 'inwardly,' " he then adds in parentheses, "because unruliness directed outwards inevitably brings on unruliness directed inwards."[50] Buber is warning that the outward injustice toward the Arabs not only harms them but will also have damaging consequences inside the new nation. Far from securing its future and safety, it will threaten its inner cohesion, bringing havoc, or "unruliness," in its train. Not only will the nation be the object of attack ("what nation will allow itself to be demoted without a fight?"), but, *by the mere fact of becoming a normal nation*, it will corrupt its inner life and will not survive.

Almost before the first shot was fired in 1948, Buber is suggesting both that Israel will be the object of aggression *and* that it will fail in its attempt to locate the aggressor purely on the outside. There is a crucial lesson here—criticizing Israel does not involve denying that it has enemies. Violence will come home to roost. In psychoanalytic parlance, the nation will fail to project. Seeing the enemy as outside threat only, Israel was sowing the seeds of long-term damage within. "Everything that did stay to challenge Israel," writes Edward Said in his essay "Zionism from the Standpoint of Its Victims," "was viewed not as something *there*, but as something *outside* Israel and Zionism bent on its destruction—from the outside."[51] One effect of course has been to render virtually invisible, or nonexistent as equal citizens, the Israeli Palestinians inside the nation. In September 2003, the Or Commission Report recommended, "The State of Israel has an interest in acting to erase the stain of discrimination against the Arab citizens."[52]

This is not, it should be stressed, the kind of criticism that bemoans the nation's subsequent betrayal of itself (a betrayal represented for many by the occupation of 1967). It is a far more radical critique. For Buber, the soul of the nation was forfeit from the day of its creation: "We have full independence, a state and all that appertains to it," Buber writes even more urgently in the following year, "but where is the nation in the state? And where is that nation's spirit?"[53] Which is not to say, it might need stressing, that Israel should cease to exist, but that the nation will perhaps survive only if it takes the fullest measure of this founding dilemma. Today, David Grossman makes the same link as did Buber between inward and outer havoc, between blindness and injustice. He makes a similar plea. The average Israeli, he writes in his dispatches from Jerusalem, refuses introspection, dreading the "disconcerting and menacing emotions it might provoke": "He dreads that they will kindle disquieting questions about the justice of his actions."[54]

If Zionism taps the unconscious, as Herzl, Hess, Pinsker, and Nordau all state in their different ways, then it seems to me that what Buber is almost saying is that *it should stay there*. An intangible dimension, spiritual and ethical, should give to this new collective being its shape. "Setting a true political goal," he writes in "Politics and Morality" in 1945, "always plumbs the depths of history and taps the primary forces which determine the life and death of peoples."[55] Again, this ethical dimension has nothing to do with Ben-Gurion's trumpeting the unique moral mission of Israel (which leads in its worst forms to the insistence voiced repeatedly by a number of those I interviewed in 2002, such as Zalman Shoval, former Israeli ambassador to the United States, that America supports Israel because as nations they share a unique moral character).

As I see it, Buber is lifting into the realm of politics the complex relations that hold between unconscious and conscious life. Freud had a formula for the aims of analysis—"Wo es war soll ich werden"—that James Strachey notoriously translated in the Standard Edition as "Where Id was there Ego shall be."[56] To which Jacques Lacan offered the countertranslation "There where *it* was so should, must, *I* come to be."[57] For Lacan, far from aiming to raise the unconscious into the realm of the all-knowing ego, which believes itself to be the sole measure of the universe, psychoanalysis should expose any such mastery as delusion. The "I" (no Ego) should cede before the unpredictable movements, the intangible processes, of the unconscious. Strachey's formula tries to normalize the mind. The ego, like the normal nation, carves out its identity. Buber quite explicitly makes the link: "The typical individual of our times," he wrote in his 1939 lecture "The Spirit of Israel and the World of Today," "holds fast to *his expanded ego, his nation*."[58] Similarly Hans Kohn would argue that Zionism, which should have offered a new model of nationhood, has fallen prey to the "*naïve and self-limited egoism* of sacred faith."[59] The nation should not be normal. Instead of owning others or itself, instead of battening down, fixing itself, knowing and owning too much, let it slip between analogies: the spirit, Buber writes, should build the life "like a dwelling or like flesh."

What would a nation look like constituted on some such terms? If this is messianism, it is a far cry from the messianism on which the nation has predominantly fashioned itself.[60] Utopian but resolutely antiapocalyptic, Buber's Zionism was not political Zionism but Zionism devoted to the life of the spirit, and, drawing on the Hasidic tradition, to the sanctification of everyday life. "The grand Eastern Jewish creation of Hasidism," writes Arnold Zweig in 1920, "pours into the most prosaic of daily activities, into the most immediate call of the day"[61] (on this Buber and Scholem parted ways—for Scholem, Buber's vision was too mundane, too much a dilution of messianic belief). Much follows from this. Although Buber was undoubtedly proposing intensive Jewish settlement of Arab land, such a Zionism does not require the ever increasing ingathering of the exiles: "We need for this land as many Jews as it is possible economically to absorb, but not in order to establish a majority against a minority."[62] Nor the denial of the Arab's political rights: "Jewish immigration must not cause the political status of the present inhabitants to deteriorate."[63] Famously Balfour had spoken of the civic and religious but not political rights of the "existing non-Jewish communities in Palestine," whereas the program of the Ichud, or League for Arab-Jewish Rapprochement to which Buber was a signatory, listed as its first aim "[g]overnment in Palestine based upon equal political rights for the two peoples." Nor the conquering of the land: "we are not obliged to conquer the land, for no danger is in store for our spiritual essence or our way of life from the population of the land."[64]

Concretely, what Buber proposed was not partition, which he saw as a "slicing" or breaking apart of the land, but a "covenant" of two independent nations with equal political rights, "united in the enterprise of developing their common homeland and in the federal management of shared matters."[65] The only thing to be sanctified for Buber is "work in common," by which he means in common with the Arabs—not the land, not the state (there should not be a sovereign state), only the slow pacings of daily tasks. For Buber, writing in 1948, the fact that Zionism failed this opportunity, made itself sovereign so as to enter into the world of nations, is nothing short of a political and spiritual catastrophe: "This sort of 'Zionism' blasphemes the name of Zion."[66]

Compare Herzl: "I have already drafted . . . the entire plan. I know everything required for it. Money, money, money, and more money; means of transportation, provisions for a vast multitude, maintenance of discipline, organisation . . . treaties with heads of state . . . the construction of new and splendid dwelling places. And beforehand, a prodigious propaganda . . . pictures, songs . . . a flag."[67]

Or compare Weizmann, in whose discourse the plea for normality is thunderous: "the greatest challenge to the creative forces of the Jewish people, its redemption from the *abnormalities* of exile"; "scattered among foreign cultures . . . our life displays something *abnormal*";"a decisive step towards *normality* and true emancipation"; "our relations to the other races and nations would become more *normal*"; "We shall revert to *normal* . . . 'like unto all the nations.' "[68] For Buber, on the contrary, the nation becomes normal—in this he is very close to psychoanalysis—at the cost of perverting itself.

Hans Kohn, one of Buber's closest disciples and friends, had been a devoted Zionist since 1909, when he had joined the Bar Kochba student organization in Prague; he had arrived in Palestine in 1923. Explaining his decision to resign from the Zionist Organization after the Arab riots of 1929, he writes, "Such events are eye-openers and call for decisions, the urgency of which we fail to appreciate in 'normal' times."[69] For Kohn, normality veils the truth. It is a cover for the incipient violence of the burgeoning state: "We pretend to be innocent victims. Of course the Arabs attacked us in August. Since they have no armies, they could not obey the rules of war."[70] "We are obliged," he insists, "to look into the deeper causes of this revolt," such as the fact that we have not "even once made a serious attempt at seeking through negotiations the consent of the indigenous peoples" (compare Sharon, refusing even the possibility of a negotiated settlement and unilaterally withdrawing from Gaza today).[71] Even more strongly, Buber had stated, "on several occasions when peace seemed to come within our reach, we did much to prevent it"; although this did not stop him from criticizing the Arab "blindness" on the same issue of peace.[72]

Writing of the suppression of the Arab revolt, Kohn then warns against a falsely triumphant "victorious peace": "Just like the powers in the [First] World War, we have declared that we would gladly make peace if only we were strong enough."[73] Such strength, he suggests, is illusory. It will have to feed on itself. Politics in this guise is both superficial (fails to look into the "deeper cause" of this revolt) and endless. Interminable, violence will inscribe itself into the heart of the nation: "I believe that it will be possible to hold Palestine and continue to grow for a long time. This will be done first with British aid and then later with the help of our own bayonets—shamefully called *Haganah* [ie defense]—clearly because we have no faith in our own policy. But by that time we will not be able to do without the bayonets."[74] Looking back in the 1960s, Kohn explains, in an essay called "Zionism," that it was from A. D. Gordon that he drew his critique of the militarism of what was to become the Israeli state: "A people cannot be 'redeemed,' Gordon taught, by political success, even less by military victory, but only by the spiritual and moral rebirth of the individual."[75] Kohn has predicted that a nation investing itself in military power will be unable to restrain itself.

Like Buber, from whom he takes his inspiration—his essay "Nationalism" is dedicated to Buber—Kohn wants *another* type of nationalism, one that reaches, in his words, "for the stars"; neither "deadly drug" nor "hypocritical camouflage" for state needs and collective power, it will be "more loving," "more attached to the life of the individual" ("the most private and hidden essence of mankind").[76] Kohn arrives at his vision after the dark night of the First World War, which he saw as the "witch's orgy" of the nation-state.[77] He therefore invested in Zionism a belief in a new form of nationhood that would make national war "as impossible as the religious fanaticism of Saint Bartholomew's Night."[78] Similarly Virginia Woolf proclaimed in 1927, "Can't you see that nationality is over?" As Hermione Lee, Woolf's biographer, comments in parentheses after this quotation, "They would all spend the next fourteen years seeing the flaws of this argument."[79] But the analysis, even if not the utopian prediction, still holds today. For Kohn, nations were lifting from religious creeds the dangers of territorial expansion and authoritarian violence. In an ideal future, nations must therefore—here he anticipates David Hartman—shed the aura of the sacred: "The sacred rights of the nation . . . will be as incomprehensible as the military and murderous fury released by a disputed interpretation of a Biblical word or form of the sign of the cross."[80]

Like Woolf, Kohn was wrong in his hopes of what was to come. But it is one of the ironic strengths of his analysis that all its central terms—sacred, violent fury, militarism, religious fanaticism—should return to the heart of Israel's future struggle both with its neighbors and with itself (the "*slow but steady*" infiltration of fundamentalism into civic life). At a roundtable meeting of Israelis and European Jews, organized by the Jewish organization Hanadiv and held in Canisy, northern France, in January 2003, leading *Ha'aretz* journalist Daniel Ben-Simon observed that up to the outbreak of the second intifada a crucial discussion was taking place inside Israel about the relationship between a secular and a religious future for the country—or, as he put it, between democracy and clerical fascism. Now it has simply stopped (Arabic has also been taken off the school curriculum).

If Kohn's vision is, as for Buber, a form of messianism that "redeems the world," it is also—again like that of Buber—resolutely antiapocalyptic, seeing its destiny, not in the apotheosis, but in a sacrifice, of self.[81] Like Buber, Kohn distinguishes between a nation as something "inwardly experienced" ("a group of people linked together through a common descent and common or similar historical destinies") and the nation as a state "bound to the external principle of territory by politics and government" ("A relentless slash cuts away everything that is politics, state, or economy").[82] But Kohn goes even further than Buber in plumbing the psychic dimension—the compelling and dangerous force—of nationalism in its modern guise. This passage, worth quoting in full, could almost have been lifted out of Freud's *The Future of an Illusion*:

> The enormous suffering of existence, the enigma of life staring at us eternally, the plethora of all things and connections assaulting us with a destructive gesticulation, the dark beast that inexplicably threatens, keeps arising within us—all these things would be unendurable if a faith, a sustaining world principle, did not bind them into unity and give them meaning and purpose, making the remote and the unsure more familiar through the threads of myth.[83]

Nationalism, the wrong kind, the kind that has become "absolute," "an idol," allows you the illusion of mastering the unmasterable: the enigma of life, destructive gesticulations, the dark beast (for Freud, the terrors of nature, the cruelty of Fate, the sufferings imposed by civilization).[84] It allows you, like the ego, to believe you could be sufficient unto yourself. Similarly, Judah Leon Magnes, first president of the Hebrew University of Jerusalem, another dissenting voice, warned in 1930 in an article interrogatively entitled "Like All the Nations?": "There is the *Wille zur Macht*, the state, the army, the frontiers . . . now we are to be masters in our own home."[85]

"Must not," Freud asks, "the assumptions that determine our political regulations be called illusions as well?"—for Kohn, one of the worst illusions is that of "national sovereign independence," the belief that a nation could be based on the "non-intervention of the 'foreigner' in 'our' affairs."[86] Freud had famously argued in *Moses the Man*, his last major work, that the founder of the Jewish people had been an Egyptian. Edward Said's recent analysis of Freud's text as offering to the modern world the idea of a nation created by a foreigner would then place Freud in this early Zionist lineage of critique.[87] The vision of an isolated nationhood, Kohn writes, is an aberration, a "ghostly phantom."[88] We can gauge just how radical this is by comparing it with Leon Pinsker, for whom it is the Jews without a homeland who are the "ghosts," "the dead walking among the living": "We wish to be a nation like the others."[89] For Kohn, the far greater danger comes when a nation, cut off from the world around it, tries to wrap itself anxiously, defensively, around its own core: "we will not be able to do without the bayonets." In 1948, the army of the new state united the Haganah, which drew its troops from the Zionist movements devoted to pioneering and communal living, and the Irgun, the paramilitary organization that aspired to Jewish control over all of Transjordan and Palestine. Buber was aghast: "The Israeli army, elements that are [physically and spiritually] rooted in the land and those that are not, mingle with each other," wrote Buber, "*stand up as a wall, conquer, vanquish.*"[90]

From the beginning, writes Arendt in her 1944 essay "Zionism Reconsidered," Zionism wanted, more than anything, "utopian national independence."[91] But nations are not independent. To be a law (race, faith) unto yourself is a myth. Dramatically, Israel has offered the spectacle of that illusion—the belief and its necessary failure—playing itself out on the world's stage. Not for the first time, there is something fundamental about nationhood that Zionism, so determined and yet fumbling in the dark, *allows us to see.* "He did not realise," Arendt writes of Herzl, "that the country he dreamt of did not exist, that there was no place on earth where a people could live like the organic national body that he had in mind and that the real historical development of a nation does not take place inside the closed walls of a biological entity."[92]

"Paradoxical as it may sound," she argues, "it was precisely because of this nationalist misconception of the inherent independence of a nation that the Zionists ended up making the Jewish national independence entirely dependent on the material interests of another nation."[93] If nationalism is "bad enough" when it trusts in "nothing but the rude force of the nation," a nationalism dependent on the force of a foreign nation is "certainly worse."[94] Arendt warns, "[T]he anti-Semitism of tomorrow will assert that Jews not only profiteered from the presence of the foreign big powers in that region but actually plotted and hence are guilty of the consequences."[95] "Only folly," she concludes, "could dictate a policy which trusts a distant imperial power for protection, while alienating the good will of neighbours."[96] Israel, as Arendt also predicted, would become utterly reliant on America. "We feel our battle is with America," Ramallah politician Ramadan Safi told me in 2002: "the tanks are American, the guns are American, the fighters are American."[97]

It is one of the defining problems of Zionism that it imported into the Middle East a Central European concept of nationhood in the throes of decline. This was a concept of organic nationhood, founded on ethnicity and blood (or "land, descent and the dead"). For Moses Hess, ancient Judaism had in fact been the first such group in human history—romantic nationalism was therefore at once the legacy and destiny of the Jewish people. It was of course a myth, and as the century unfolded, the Jews, above all other people, would be its victim. Writing seventy years after the publication of *Der Judenstaat*, historian J. L. Talmon of the Hebrew University of Jerusalem commented, "Little did Hess, Mazzini, Mickiewicz and their like know that in endowing nationalism with the dimension of a Salvationist religion, and in transferring to it so much of the Socialist appeal, they were unwittingly offering a rationale to that type of racial, exclusive nationalism, which Hess so abhorred among the Germans, and indeed to anti-Semitism, in both its racial and social versions."[98] Israel inscribes at its heart the very version of nationhood from which the Jewish people had had to flee.

Furthermore, at the very moment when Israel was created to secure the future of the Jewish people, this version of statehood revealed, not only its inherent dangers, but its radical inability to defend the very principles on which it had once been built. Like Kohn, Arendt traces the beginning of this failure, which reaches its climax for the Jews in the Second World War, to the catastrophe of the First: "As for nationalism," she continues, "it never was more evil nor more fiercely defended than since it became apparent that this once great and revolutionary principle of the national organisation of peoples could no longer either guarantee true sovereignty of the people within, or establish a just relationship among different peoples beyond, the national borders."[99] This is nationalism, in the words of Tom Nairn, trapped in "the essentialist cage of regimented identity, flag-worship and armour-plated community."[100] National faith of this kind becomes belligerent and expansive because it is so vulnerable and so raw, defending boundaries of the body and mind that do not exist. For that very reason, it "permits and excuses anything" (the words of Hans Kohn, who could just as well be describing the politics of the preemptive war on terror today).[101]

Picking up her pen like Buber in May 1948, Arendt predicts with uncanny prescience the future of the new nation after its victory in the coming war:

> The "victorious" Jews would live surrounded by an entirely hostile Arab population, secluded inside ever-threatened borders, absorbed with physical self-defense to a degree that would submerge all other interests and activities. The growth of a Jewish culture would cease to be the concern of the whole people; social experiments would have to be discarded as impractical luxuries; political thought would center around military strategy; economic development would be determined exclusively by the need of war.[102]

Explaining his refusal to serve in the occupied territories, Lieutenant Yaniv Iczkovitz states: "The Labor party is coming apart, and Meretz, the Israeli social democratic peace party, can be neither seen nor heard. . . . The chairman of the opposition is the chairman of silence. The biggest mistake of the left is its preoccupation with security issues. . . . It's a sin that began with the establishment of the state."[103] "Our country is going into a decline, nearing a catastrophe in all areas of economy, politics and social services and security," Yaakov Perry, who ran Shin Bet from 1988 to 1995, commented recently. "If we continue to live by the sword, we will continue to wallow in the mud and to destroy ourselves."[104]

The nation cannot secure its own future. Surely, it is often asked, Jewish nationalism is justified by the need of the Jewish people to have a place in the world where they can feel safe? Or physically and mentally at ease—a place where, as Gordon wrote to Ahad Ha'am in 1912, the Jew does not have endlessly to check the beat of his national pulse (the second epigraph to this chapter). But the Jews are not safe in Israel today. Nor indeed at ease with themselves. Exactly as Arendt predicted, the ethos of survival "at any price"—whose emergence in the thought of the nation is the topic of the next chapter—has become brutalized and now, after thirty-seven years in the occupied territories, is placing not just the safety but the sanity of the nation at risk. "I was carried away by the possibility of acting in the most primal and impulsive manner," Staff Sergeant Liran Ron Furer says of his experience in Gaza in his book *Checkpoint Syndrome*. "Over time the behaviour . . . became normative . . . without fear of punishment and without oversight . . . a place to test our personal limits—how tough, how callous, how crazy we could be."[105]

"The question that looms," writes Ze'ev Schiff in *Ha'aretz* after the assassination of Hamas leader Sheikh Yassin in March 2004, "is whether Israel has been attacked by the virus of a crazy state."[106] According to Amir Rappaport, writing in the newspaper *Ma'ariv*, Israel's air strikes on Gaza, which came in response to eight Qassam rockets fired by the Palestinians in October in 2003, were deliberately disproportionate to convey the message to the Palestinians that "Israel has gone mad."[107] "I see terrible graffiti—racist and Kahanist—that we accept offhandedly," writes Avraham Burg, former speaker of the Knesset and member of the Labor Party; the settlers and the right wing have left no "place that is not affected by the nationalist consciousness."[108]

In their different ways, in the dialogic space that runs between Buber, Arendt, and Kohn, I hear all of them arguing that Zionism might have created a form of nationhood that would slash away politics, face its own dark beast, make room for the foreigner in its midst (or, even more radically perhaps, see itself as the stranger for the Arabs in Palestine). For a brief moment, Zionism had the chance of molding a nation that would be not an "expanded ego" but something else. At the opening of his essay "Nationalism," Kohn describes how "shifts of consciousness" are always accompanied by "deep shocks," creating a time of "disquiet, tension, isolation, dissociation"; such processes are "obscure," "ambivalent," "uncertain."[109] He could be describing glimpses of the unconscious, those moments—dreams, slips, symptoms—when the unconscious is allowed to steal past the wires, past the defenses of the conscious mind, and makes its presence felt. Precisely because of the tragic peculiarity of Jewish history, because Jews have indeed in some sense been lost to the world—we do not have to reject Pinsker's "ghosts"—Zionism, as a unique national movement, had the opportunity to forge a model of nationhood, neither belligerently nor preemptively, but ambivalent, uncertain, obscure, something closer to this disquieting and transformative space. But did not take it.

Meanwhile, the vision they all sustained for a life and nationhood held in common for Jews and Arabs is one that has returned to the center of debate inside Israel today. Partly out of fear—if Israel holds on to the territories, Jews "risk becoming a minority in their own land" (this fear is seen by many to be the only driving force behind Sharon's Gaza plan);[110] partly, however, because it is felt that the settlements have rendered a two-state solution nonviable, and that the only way forward is for Israel to become the state of all its citizens. The idea of a binational solution is by no means widely accepted—for its opponents it precisely spells the destruction of a Jewish state. But it has some barely known historic precedents, moments of cohabitation and cooperation between Jews and Arabs in Mandate Palestine, against the drift of their hardening respective nationalisms, recently uncovered by Ilan Pappe: "From a historiographical point of view," he writes, "the impression left is of an alternative history."[111] In 1948, Herbert Samuels wrote to Jan Smuts of South Africa, "The right alternative [to partition] is a provision for Jewish and Arab representative bodies based upon the actual facts of the situation, that is to say, upon the existence of communities that cannot be segregated geographically either into states, provinces or cantons."[112] Today the binational idea finds some unlikely adherents. For Daniel Gavron—"mainstream, orthodox Labour Zionist," as he describes himself, whose book *The Other Side of Despair: Jews and Arabs in the Promised Land* appeared in Israel in 2003—such a vision follows logically from the multiethnic character of the ancient world: "King David, if the Bible is to be believed, conquered Jerusalem from the Jebusites and then shared the city with them. He made use of

Canaanite officials, had a Hittite general, enjoyed good relations with the Phoenicians, and (after some bloody conflicts with them) deployed Philistine units in his army, the Cherethites and Pelethites."[113]

When Hannah Arendt expresses her fears for the growth of Jewish culture, or Martin Buber talks of an organic center, they may well have been thinking of Ahad Ha'am, for whom Jewish culture was the sole raison d'être of a homeland in Palestine. Ahad Ha'am, who took the pen name "one of the people," was born Asher Ginzberg in Skvire, in the Russian Ukraine. Although little known today outside Israel, inside the country some of his writings are still taught at school. They were also read by Noam Chomsky in his youth. Most famous for his plea for Palestine to become a "spiritual centre" for world Jewry, he was, like Buber and Kohn—the latter edited a selection of his writings—deeply suspicious of the idea of statehood. On publication of the Balfour Declaration, which as Weizmann's "intimate adviser" he had played a part in formulating, he commented,

> The British Government promised to facilitate the establishment in Palestine of a National Home *for* the Jewish people, and not, as was suggested, the reconstitution of Palestine as the National Home *of* the Jewish people.[114]

Much hangs on that distinction between "for" and "of." If Balfour meant that the Jews had the "historic right" to build their national home in Palestine, it also meant "a *negation of the power of that right to override the right of the present inhabitants, and to make the Jewish people the sole ruler in the country.*"[115] Kohn had warned of incipient Arab nationalism: "The Arab national movement is growing and will continue to grow."[116] But Ahad Ha'am was one of the rare critical voices to speak of Arab national aspirations in positive terms: "This country is their national home," he wrote to Weizmann in 1918, "and they too have the right to develop a national power to the best of their abilities" (the topic was rarely broached even by Brit Shalom).[117]

Ahad Ha'am's reputation as Jewish nationalism's major internal critic dates from his first 1891 visit to Palestine. "What I have seen," he wrote in his article "The Truth from Palestine," is the "concrete truth . . . of which I wish to reveal a bit—the ugliest bit."[118] Ahad Ha'am presents himself as the purveyor of the (ugliest) truth. Variously described as the "first philosopher of Zionism," "foremost exponent of a humanistic, liberal Zionism," and "disturber of the peace," Ahad Ha'am was also the first Jewish nationalist to recognize the darker side to the relationship between Arabs and Jews in Palestine.[119] How, he asked, in a scathing review of Herzl's *Altneuland*, could the New Society obtain sufficient land for Jews from all over the world if the arable land that previously belonged to the Arabs remained in their hands as before?[120] Each paragraph of "The Truth from Palestine" began with the phrase "We are accustomed to believe"; for instance, that Palestine is empty, whereas in fact arable land is at a premium and there is very little left. "We are accustomed to believe that all the Arabs are desert savages."[121] It was a role he maintained. In 1913, he answered a letter from Hebrew writer Moshe Smilansky on the settlers' treatment of the Arabs, specifically on the boycott of Arab labor: "If it is so now, what will be our relation to the others if in truth we shall achieve 'at the end of time' power in Eretz Israel? If this be the 'Messiah', I do not wish to see his coming."[122]

"One of the people," Ahad Ha'am sets himself up as a type of prophet (or analyst) speaking truth to a power in gestation, to a state, not already established and glib in its empowerment, but in the very throes of creating itself. In Ahad Ha'am's writing, as I see it, Zionism diagnoses or *reads itself*.

Ahad Ha'am was Herzl's most articulate critic. To invoke the title of one of his earliest and most influential pieces of writing, he thought Herzl was going about things "the wrong way" (too much money, too many flags). It was not just that Ahad Ha'am promoted a spiritual rather than political embodiment of nationalism; it was also that, like Buber, he thought that the path to nationalism involved a complex negotiation of historical and psychic time. Things started to go wrong when a new, revived, belief in the right of the Jews to be a "single" people transformed itself, with seemingly miraculous efficiency, into deeds: "The friends of the idea raised a shout of victory, and cried in exultation. Is not this a thing unheard-of, that an idea so young has strength to force its way into the world of action?"[123] But the "shout of victory" and cry "of exultation" were mistaken. Triumphalism is always a form of magical thinking or self-deceit: "Every victory involves a defeat and a death."[124] Similarly, Scholem had written to Walter Benjamin in 1931, "We were victorious too early."[125] Impatient, Jewish nationalism, finding it had the strength to force its way, became incapable of deferring itself. It is, he writes, a peculiarity of the Hebrew language that it has no present tense: "Israel has never lived in the present."[126] In their rush to the future, the Jewish people were failing to subsist in the slow interstices of everyday time (where Buber located the sacred).[127]

Moses was his hero. It is impossible not to read his long essay on the Jewish leader as a critique of Herzl: "He knows that signs and wonders and visions of God can arouse a momentary enthusiasm, but cannot create a new heart. . . . So he summons all his patience to the task of bearing the troublesome burden of his people and training it by slow steps."[128] In a way Moses's greatest quality becomes his failure. That he did not enter the Promised Land, that he had to face the "utter, fathomless, degradation of his people" and "tear out of his heart a splendid hope."[129] Today, although the future, as utopian promise, is on everyone's lips, Ahad Ha'am believed that the possibility of a real, more difficult future had been "forgotten," as the Jewish people sped toward their felt destiny in unseemly haste. Instead nirvana had taken its place. For Ahad Ha'am, the danger facing the Jewish people from political Zionism was a ruthless self-idealization that will brook no disappointment and knows no bounds (in Magnes's terms, the "*Wille zur Macht*," in Arendt's, Herzl's "will to reality" or "furious will to action at any price").[130] "Everything must be done immediately!" Herzl had written to Moritz Güdemann in 1895; "that too is part of my plan."[131]

In *Der Judenstaat*, Herzl had deliberately raised the expectations of the earliest pioneers by insisting that only those would depart for Palestine who "are sure thereby to improve their position."[132] "To attract the

Jews to the land," he stated in conversation with Hirsch in 1895, "you would have to tell them a fable about how to strike gold. By way of fantastic example, you might say: whoever ploughs, sows and reaps will find gold in every sheaf. Nearly the truth in fact."[133] For Ahad Ha'am, in this scenario, the "demon of egoism," the flush of individual self-interest, substitutes for the more complex historical and cultural affinities of the group, which became vulnerable when, as was often the case with the earliest emigrants to Palestine, personal expectations were not met.[134] Losing touch with its historical memory—"the chain" uniting "all the generations"—political Zionism wrongly promised too much: "a complete and absolute solution of the Jewish problem in all its aspects."[135] In the process, it made the mistake of demanding actualization, for each and every one of its actors, in the here and now (I want results). Note how in this case the idea of a chain of ancestral memories forging a link to the land—the idea so often voiced to justify the occupation of "Eretz Israel"—leads to the opposite of a violent claim upon it. What matters are the group's inner or, as Buber would put it, "inward" relations. Jewish nationalism must take out the ego. Overanxious to realize its ambitions, the ego always tends to get carried away, to move too fast. Paradoxically, Jewish nationalism will come into being only if—as a dream of seizing the land, ruling the Arabs, economically prospering—it abolishes itself. Ahad Ha'am's proposal is both modest and slow (this is not Weizmann calling for the long, but finally proprietorial, cultivation of the territory). Offering himself as the group analyst of Zionism—to the various descriptions already offered, I would like to add one more—he puts a question. How do you make a nation pause for thought?

"The human mind," he writes, "has laws of its own not always consistent with logic."[136] It is a central part of Ahad Ha'am's project to trace those laws, which dominate "not only the judgement but the memory," as they impact on collective life.[137] "A people," he recognizes, "cannot live on logic"; they are indeed guided, in the words of Herzl, by "imponderables" that float "in thin air."[138] Ahad Ha'am can be seen as taking up Herzl's formula—for Herzl a political opportunity to relish—where he left off. If not a redemptive, or even apocalyptic, fulfillment of self, then it must be asked: what alternative version of Jewish selfhood should Zionism be trying to promote? In what does, or should, a political identity consist? What allows a man, or a group, to believe in itself? All questions, Ahad Ha'am's writings reveal, that are at the heart of the most fundamental political disagreements about the future of Palestine.

"When a man says "I," Ahad Ha'am writes in "Past and Future," "he is thinking of that inner spirit, or force, which in some hidden manner unites all the impressions and memories of the past with all his desires and hopes for the future, and makes of the whole one single, complete, organic entity."[139] The organic "I," which is not, note, the same as the individual ego, matches the organic center of Judaism, which the homeland in Palestine will bring to life. Ahad Ha'am takes this vision of psychic unity from the works of French psychiatrist Frédéric Paulhan—whose study of the growth of Darwin's creative personality he used as the basis for his own discussion of Moses: "a mind which reached an almost perfect unity."[140] "The mind," writes Paulhan, "is or tends to be a unified and coordinated whole."[141]

But the mind is also a palimpsest, its inheritance imperishable. Latent within us, we carry the traces of those parts of the personality that our predecessors inhibited and that never completely disappear: "we are always to some extent what we once were before or what our ancestors were before us."[142] Ahad Ha'am's vision of an organic center for Judaism is therefore mapped directly onto a theory of the mind as at once unified and multiply shaded, a mind filled with the inhibitions of our forefathers, the traces of our ancestors, the fragments of the past. You would be hard pressed to draw from this vision of the psyche or inner life any foundation whatsoever for the too hasty, surefire political will. There is a continuity here—Jewishness cannot survive without it—but it is precarious, treading on ghostly, unmasterable, ground. "Unity," writes Paulhan in his analysis of Darwin, "remains only an ideal."[143] Even the harmonious mind bears the scars of its former struggles.

In Paulhan's model, the mind is endlessly at work. At every instant, psychic phenomena awaken inside us, develop, and disappear, giving rise to others in their place, entering into play often despite ourselves and without our knowledge. "There is," he writes in his 1905 *Lies of Character*, no part of our soul "that is not disputed, fought, denied by another."[144] In our ideals we constantly lie to ourselves. "Do not seek precision and stability in psychic life; the facts of the mind are more mobile, fluctuating, and restless than the waves of the sea."[145] A truly organic center of Judaism would not make the mistake, like a declaration of statehood, of thinking that either the mind or the soul could come to rest.

At moments Ahad Ha'am's view of subjectivity is truly, and often disturbingly, psychoanalytic before its time. "Every civilised man who is born and bred in an orderly state of society," he writes in his 1892 essay "Two Masters," "lives all his life in the condition of hypnotic subject, unconsciously subservient to the will of others."[146] The opening of the essay is worth quoting:

> Familiar as we now are with the phenomena of hypnotism, we know that under certain conditions it is possible to induce a peculiar kind of sleep in a human being, and that, if the hypnotic subject is commanded to perform at a certain time after his awakening some action foreign to his character and wishes, he will obey the order at the appointed time. He will not know, however, that he is compelled to do so by the will and behest of another. He will firmly believe . . . that he is doing what he does of his own freewill and because he likes to do so, for various reasons which his imagination will create, in order to satisfy his own mind.[147]

The question Ahad Ha'am puts to political Zionism could be put to any form of political selfhood, any nationalism, carving out its space in the world. It is as if he were questioning the idea that the only way to forge a political life and future is to believe, unreservedly, in the force of identity, to believe that identity—this would be one version of Jewish identity—is exclusive, and, as a people, exclusively your own. Bit by bit Ahad Ha'am takes apart our pride of possession in the components that make up a self. Language and literature, religion and morality, laws and customs—these are the "media" society uses to put the individual "to sleep."[148] Inside every individual member of society, there are "thousands of hypnotic agents, whose commands are stern and peremptory"—"Such and such shall be your opinions; such and such your actions"—and which the individual "unconsciously" obeys.[149]

Nearly forty years before Freud's *Civilization and Its Discontents*, Ahad Ha'am has produced an account of the superego ferociously issuing its edicts to the unconscious mind. The fiercest edicts—"arch-hypnotisers, the all-powerful masters of the individual and society alike"—are the "men of the distant past."[150] Because they are unconscious, these voices are unanswerable. If they carry the dynasty of the ages, they are also the bearers of some of its most sinister calls. Hatred of the Jews is one of the "best-established commands of the past to the nations of Europe."[151] Our most forceful legacy comes from voices of the past that we cannot even necessarily hear speaking.

What would happen to a political or religious identity, even the most binding, if it could see itself as contingent, as something that might have taken another path? Can you be devoted to an identity—or would you be differently devoted to your identity—if you knew it was also unsure? The priest Mortara "thunders" from his pulpit against the enemies of the Catholic faith, striving out of the depths of his "inner consciousness" to prove its righteousness and truth, but if Catholic priests had not snatched him from the arms of his Jewish mother in childhood, other "hypnotic" agents would have been "speaking through his lips with precisely the same warmth of conviction."[152] It is because deep down they are not wholly convinced, that people have to deceive themselves and lie, as Paulhan put it, in the service of their ideals. Following the Arab riots of 1936, a group of schoolchildren at the agricultural school Ben Shemen were set the question "How do you explain the troubles arising in the country over the past few weeks?" Dr. Siegfried Lehmann, director of the school, summarizes the essays: "right is on our side; good can come out of evil; the whole world and the Arabs [*sic*] will know that we wish for peace." He comments, "As in a dream, one notes the complete lack of any unpleasant reality which might risk thwarting our aspirations."[153]

Like Freud, Ahad Ha'am, citing American philosopher John Fiske, uses Copernicus to underscore the radically decentered nature of this account of subjectivity:

> It is hard to realise the startling effect of the discovery that man does not dwell at the centre of things, but is the denizen of an obscure and tiny speck of cosmical matter quite invisible amid the innumerable throng of flaming suns that make up our galaxy.[154]

For Freud, man had suffered a triple blow to the hubris of the ego: not the center of the universe, nor the origin of the species, nor master in his own psychic home. "Man does not dwell at the centre of things." In fact, as much as Freud, the passage could be Robert Louis Stevenson, who famously postulated in *The Strange Case of Dr Jekyll and Mr Hyde*, "I hazard the guess that man will be ultimately known for a mere polity of multifarious, incongruous and independent denizens."[155] The ego crumbles. In the name of *another* Judaism, neither orthodoxy nor statehood, Ahad Ha'am brings pretty much the whole apparatus of psychoanalysis—the deadly and deceptive lure of the ego, the ferocity of the superego, the unconsciously commanded subject—blazing in his train.

As if the only path open for Jewish nationalism's strongest internal critic is through the defiles of the unconscious. Jacques Lacan once said of the hysteric that the screen of the ego is strangely transparent, "there being nowhere else, as Freud has said, where the threshold between the unconscious and the conscious is lower."[156] If the hysteric is compelling, Lacan also suggests, it is because she never stops asking the most basic questions—like, for example, "Do I exist or not?" Likewise Zionism—so fragile *and* dogmatic, so ruthless with its own doubts that are yet so transparently there to see. "I am tormented by an abrupt question that will not leave me in peace," wrote early Zionist, Russian student, Haim Chisin in his diary in 1882, " 'Who are you?' I try to convince myself: 'Do I really have to be somebody?' "[157]

When I interviewed settlers Aaron and Tamara Deutsch, they insisted, as of course many settlers insist, that Israel is the land God promised to the Jews. "We wanted to join our people and our destiny, our history and our nation."[158] In his pathbreaking book *Zakhor* first published in 1982, Yosef Hayim Yerushalmi pointed out that it was a peculiarity and creation of Jewish thought that human history reveals the will and purpose of God ("the fathers of meaning in history were the Jews").[159] For the rabbinic tradition that dominated Jewish historiography for centuries, history was not a continuous and continuing chronicle of deed or event, but lifted above time as a vehicle of the sacred. It is precisely against this tradition that David Hartman makes his plea for Israeli society to end the vision of its history as divinely sanctioned and reenter the slow accommodations of political time. For the Deutsches, the world today, Israel today, fulfills the covenant of the past: "These are the roads where Abraham walked. This is where Jacob married Rachel."[160] "The Bible," as Ben-Gurion put it, "is our Mandate." Following Ahad Ha'am's account of hypnotic agency, we could describe this as ancestral belonging with a vengeance (it was precisely in their most fervent moments that the Deutsches seemed to be talking by rote). "To this day," writes journalist Nadav Shragai, the residents of Kfar Darom "feel the 'ancient voices' are a part of their daily life, and not just something to be thought of as metaphor or heritage."[161] To Yerushalmi's investigation of historical time, we might therefore add another question. Whose voice is speaking when they speak?[162]

Like all Zionists, Ahad Ha'am was troubled by the assimilation of the Diaspora Jews. If he opposed political Zionism, it was not because he thought dispersal was the only possible Jewish identity and fate (he entered into lengthy dispute with Simon Dubnow, who advocated that the Jews should become a national entity inside their respective European nations). But when he criticized assimilation, it was not, he insisted, in the name of an identity that should see itself as self-sufficient and pure. As well as hypnotic, identity was for Ahad Ha'am fundamentally mimetic (we discover ourselves by imitating the others who we are). Imitation, he wrote in his 1893 essay

"Imitation and Assimilation," is wrongly taken as the sign that a man is not "speaking out of his own inner life," whereas it is in fact the very foundation of society, without which its birth and development would not take place.[163] It is only when imitation slides into self-effacement that it leads to assimilation, a state of "neither life nor death" in which all national or communal consciousness is lost: "no community can sink to such a position as this without danger to its very existence" (the soul is "burnt out").[164]

Ahad Ha'am is struggling to produce a version of Jewish identity that, even in the Diaspora, will preserve itself. This was for him one of the main purposes of establishing a "spiritual centre of our nationality," or Jewish spiritual center in Palestine.[165] He was at pains to stress that this did not mean the center in Palestine would be spiritual only, but that it would be a spiritual center for Jewry worldwide (not all Jews, he also insisted, would have to come to Palestine). And he wants this identity free of the stifling dictates of rabbinic Orthodoxy, which produce slavish imitation in another guise. He would have been appalled by Tamara Deutsch's call for a Torah State.

I like to think that Ahad Ha'am is calling on his forebears to soften or modulate their voice (rather like psychoanalysis aiming to reduce the ferocity of the superego in the mind of a child). Jewishness, he believed, must be saved, or rather reforged in the crucible of the new homeland. But if you are meant to imbibe the spirit of the ancestors, you are not meant to be slavishly mouthing the dead. Furthermore, as evidenced by the tale of the thundering Catholic priest snatched in childhood from his Jewish mother, you may feel secure in your cultural, religious, or ethnic selfhood, but you could in fact have been anyone. People who thunder, psychoanalysis would merely add, are generally those who are least sure of themselves. We can watch Ahad Ha'am trying to create a new identity for the Jewish people, at the same time as he acknowledges with equal force that your identity is never simply your own but always comes from somewhere or somebody else. Can there be—this is a question for modern times—a form of identity that is what it is *and* everything else at once?

Out of the creative instability of Ahad Ha'am's psychological vision, something even more provisional, suggestive, starts to emerge. If identities are formed mimetically, coercively, hypnotically, they are also on the move ("more restless than the waves of the sea"). They travel. Across communities in the present as much as to the ancestors of the past. Imitation is promiscuous. As soon as different societies are brought into "closer intimacy," "fuller acquaintance" with one another, identities start to spread and to blur.[166] Imitation "widens its scope," becomes "intersocial or international."[167] No man, no nation can isolate itself. Moses "makes no distinction between man and man" but goes to the aid of strangers.[168] Remember Kohn and Arendt, for whom the greatest and most dangerous illusion was the sovereign, independent nation closing in on itself: "the non-intervention of the 'foreigner' in 'our' affairs is a dangerous phantom."[169] What would Israel look like if it acknowledged its intimate affinity with its neighbors? We are, stated Weizmann, in many respects "their cousins."[170] What would happen if Israel could recognize its links to the people who—whether in refugee camps on the borders (the putative Palestinian state), or inside the country (the Israeli Palestinians), or scattered, like many Jews still today, all over the world (the Palestinian diaspora)—are in fact, psychically as well as politically, in its midst?

What finally emerges from Ahad Ha'am's writing is a type of psychic manifesto, not just for Zionism, but for modern times. We need, he insists, to be open. We need, not just to imbibe, but to *understand*, the spirit of the ages (we should study and read). "The student of the spiritual life of mankind," he writes in "Ancestor Worship," "has no concern with good and evil, wisdom or folly."[171] He becomes the "spiritual incarnation of the souls of all the ages," a conduit to everything in the past.[172] We are not "better" than our ancestors; we are "different." We do not rush to judgment. We allow the capacity for evil its place in our own minds: "there is nothing so barbarous, so evil, that the human mind cannot accept it and foster it, given suitable conditions."[173] Compare again Freud: "no one can really know how far he is good or wicked."[174] Once you say this, you stop thundering from the pulpit. Identity ceases to be a creed. We have a monopoly on neither righteousness nor truth, "and consequently many of the sacred truths of every generation must become falsehoods and absurdities in the next."[175] Nor, perhaps above all, on judgment: "they who judge today will not escape scot free from the tribunal of tomorrow."[176]

It is important not to idealize Ahad Ha'am. He was notoriously elitist, autocratic—Bnei Moshe, the organization that he founded in Odessa in 1889 to foster Jewish spiritual self-development, foundered under pressure of his exacting requirements. Unlike Buber, he did argue that the Jews must be a majority in Palestine. He could be racist. He objected, for example, to the suggestion in *Altneuland* that a homeland for the Jews should lead to liberation and nationhood for the "negroes" of Africa. But he throws out a set of urgent questions to Jewish nationalism that still need, or need perhaps even more, to be thought about today. What effect would it have on the dominant rhetoric of the Israeli state if it allowed its own capacity for evil? What would happen if it allowed that it was being hypnotized, coerced, by the ancestral voices from which, it insists, the nation's authority stems? Or if it allowed that it might once have been snatched from the arms of a mother of another faith? Or that it was sleepwalking? Or that its boundaries should not be fixed against the enemy but should loosen to allow a place for the stranger whom Moses went to save? Or that it might be answerable for its activities in the occupied territories today before the tribunal of tomorrow? "People listened to the victim and they listened to the politicians," writes Staff Sergeant Liran Ron Furer, "but this voice that says: I did this, we did things that were wrong—crimes actually—that's a voice I didn't hear."[177]

Speaking of Operation Defensive Shield, in which the army responded to suicide bombing by razing the town of Jenin, army chief of staff Lieutenant General Moshe Ya'alon "told some of his soldiers that he did not care if the army 'looked like lunatics.' " Ya'alon is not consistent, at moments calling for a change in Israeli policy on the grounds that its treatment of Palestinian civilians is fomenting terror, at others giving public seminars arguing that Hamas, Islamic Jihad, and other organizations should be lured into a clash with the IDF and killed en masse.[178]

At the heart of the army, voices—the refuseniks now include Black Hawk helicopter and F-16 fighter pilots, as well as members of the elite Sayaret Matkal, Israel's special forces—are crying out that Israel's belief in its own moral destiny, under pressure of the occupation, is slowly turning inward and imploding.[179] "No one," writes ultra-Orthodox Yehuda Shaul—who, after serving in Gaza, curated an exhibition of photographs of human rights abuses by the army in Hebron—"returns from the territories without messing up his head."[180] "The moment I drove the tractor into the camp, something switched in my head. I went mad," writes Moshe Nissim, the D9 tank operator in Jenin in 2003, "I wanted to destroy everything."[181] "It's a sin," writes Lieutenant Iczkovitz, "that began with the establishment of the state."[182] In the new homeland, the Jew—as Herzl, Gordon, and so many believed—would be a "natural wholesome human being who is true to himself."[183]

In his essay "Politics and Morality" of 1945, Martin Buber spoke of the Jewish need for an "organic centre," a desire and indeed a phrase he shared with Ahad Ha'am, and then proceeded to draw an ethical boundary around what was permissible to achieve it: "I seek to protect my nation by keeping it from false limits."[184] Remember Buber always called himself a Zionist, unlike Kohn, who ceased to do so, and Arendt, who did so only with immense qualifications (by the 1960s, Buber's involvement in the publication *Ner*, which fought against military rule in the Arab areas, further sharpened his critique). If, Buber writes, one has the "intention of driving people who are bound to the soil out of their homeland," then the limits of the permissible have been breached: "I shall never agree that in this matter it is possible to justify injustice by pleading values or destinies." And he continues, "if there is a power of righteousness that punishes evil-doing, it will intervene here and react."[185]

Buber was right but also wrong. What he names explicitly as a "transfer of population," the expulsion of the Palestinians, took place with no answering intervention, no retribution, from above (the political narrative will be the topic of the final chapter to follow). I read Buber as saying that what leads nations astray—what would lead the new Jewish nation astray—is false conviction. As soon as destinies and values become secure possessions, they serve to legitimate power. Omnipotent, they start to corrupt themselves. When he wrote this essay in 1945, the full extent of the destruction of European Jewry was known—not the easiest of moments to set limits when all human limits had been crossed. But perhaps for that very reason it was all the more imperative to do so. In its statement of July 1945, published in *Herut* (Freedom), the Irgun attacked Buber's organization, the Ichud:

> We reject the morality of the observers [*ha-tzofim*], the professors of Mt. Scopus [*Har-Hatzofim*]. We the flesh of the flesh of the slaughtered [Jews of Europe], we the blood of their blood. And what is more important, we the spirit of

> the spirit of the martyrs of Israel in the past, the present and the future. . . . In matters of supreme importance we do not and will not know compromise.[186]

Perhaps the most dangerous historical moments are when a destiny seems unanswerable (the nation will not survive if it has to compromise or criticize itself). "Today reality has become a nightmare," Arendt wrote in May 1946, "horrible beyond the scope of the human imagination."[187] The Jewish people now see themselves, as Herzl had always seen them, as surrounded by eternal enemies. "Our failure to be surprised at this development," she continues, "does not make Herzl's picture truer—it only makes it more dangerous."[188]

Naomi Chazan was until 2002 deputy speaker of the Knesset and is a member of Meretz, the party described by refusenik Lieutenant Iczkovitz as "neither seen nor heard" in this time of greatest need. When I interviewed her in Tel Aviv in 2002, she issued a caution resonant of Martin Buber in 1945. "Survival," she said, "is not a value . . . tolerance is, peace is, equality is. But survival is not a value. Survival is the means to something else."[189] I was, I admit, astounded to hear an Israeli say this. After all, Jewish survival can be seen as the cause of Israel and, in the dominant rhetoric, of everything that has happened since. My cast of characters in this chapter—Buber, Kohn, Arendt, and Ahad Ha'am—all believed, however, that survival, however urgent, indeed desperate for those who lived to 1945, should become not the rationale of statehood but the means to something else.

Then, as now, the issue was justice. As early as 1932, Buber had offered his warning to a Zionism that would achieve its aims "at any price': "It may however be characteristic of Zion that it *cannot* be built 'with every possible means,' but only *bemishpat* (Isaiah, 1:27), only 'with justice'."[190] In March 2004, Rabbis for Human Rights took out a full-page advertisement in *Ha'aretz* to express support for their colleague Rabbi Arik Ascherman, on trial in Jerusalem for trying to prevent the demolition of Palestinian homes. Returning to the vision I have tried to evoke here, they make their appeal to an earlier, lost, image of Zion: "Zion will only be redeemed through justice and those who can return to her through acts of righteousness."[191]

In his book *Israel and Palestine Out of the Ashes: The Search for Jewish Identity in the Twenty-First Century*, Marc Ellis suggests that Jews often do not know that there was this history of dissent which has been "forgotten or deliberately buried."[192] Most simply, I have wanted to revive it. To show that Zionism was not one thing, that it knew itself better than it thinks. To read these writers, alongside the dominant voices of Israeli statehood we looked at in the previous chapter, is to be confronted with something like a split between lethal identification and grievous disenchantment; as if the State of Israel were offering its citizens and the rest of the world only the options of idealization or radical dissent. It is also to be struck with an overwhelming sense of a moment missed, of voices silenced, of an argument, at terrible cost, re-repressed. Today we are all still suffering the loss of their critical, insightful, vision.

Chapter 3

"Break their bones": Zionism as Politics (Violence)

At Basel . . . I gradually hounded the people into the mood for a state.

—Theodor Herzl, *Tagebücher* (September 3, 1897)[1]

We must think like a state.

—David Ben-Gurion, address to the Central Committee of the Histadrut (December 30, 1947)

We are choking with shame about what is happening in Germany, in Poland, and in America, that Jews are not daring to fight back. We do not belong to that Jewish people. . . . We do not want to be such Jews."

—David Ben-Gurion, *Memoirs*

We die from hiding our shames.

—Bernard Lazare to Theodor Herzl (February 4, 1899)

According to a legendary story, Sigmund Freud celebrated Emperor Franz Josef's refusal to confirm the anti-Semite Karl Lueger as mayor of Vienna in 1895 with an extra ration of cigars. Theodor Herzl, who had settled in Vienna in September of that year, saw no reason to celebrate. Although he entertained fantasies of challenging Lueger to a duel, he nonetheless thought the emperor's refusal was a mistake.[2] Lueger's popularity would be strengthened; race-hatred would not be quelled. Over the next two years, Lueger's victory was overturned no fewer than four times before the emperor finally, reluctantly, confirmed him in place. For many Jews in Austria it was the moment that signaled the end of an emancipatory dream. Although Lueger himself is not generally regarded as the most virulent of anti-Semites, he was nonetheless particularly skilled at exploiting the indeterminate components of fear. "Wer ein Jud' ist, bestimme Ich" ("I decide who is a Jew"), he once chillingly pronounced.[3] Throughout the last years of the decade, the *Neue Freie Presse*, the newspaper for which Herzl wrote, reported the steady increase in anti-Jewish incidents—riots in Vienna against Jewish property, large-scale anti-Jewish riots in Galicia in 1888 and in Bohemia against "pro-German" Jews the following year. Already in 1895, when the anti-Semitic factions were approaching majority status in the Austrian lower diet, Representative Schneider had called—to applause and sneering laughter from his supporters, cries of indignation from the Left—for the extermination of the Jews: "Austria will be *wunderschön* again, and good. . . . Why shouldn't this people, this God-damned rabble, be exterminated from the face of the earth?"[4]

Despite Herzl's prescience about Lueger, it is a strange fact of Zionist history that the figure responsible for launching Zionism as a political movement desired nothing so much as to be an emancipated, not to say assimilated, Jew: "I am a German Jew from Hungary," Herzl announced in his speech to the Rothschilds in 1895, "and I can never be anything but a German."[5] In fact Herzl believed he would be recognized as German only upon the creation of the Jewish state: "At present I am not recognised as a German. That will come soon, once we are over there."[6] "Through Zionism Jews will again be able to love this Germany, to which despite everything our hearts have clung."[7] Herzl's own relationship to anti-Semitism was ambivalent, to say the least: "What would you say, for example, if I did not deny that there are good aspects of anti-Semitism," he wrote in 1893 to his fiancée Julie Naschauser. "I myself would never convert [but] one must baptize Jewish boys before they are able to act against it. . . . They must disappear into the crowd."[8] In the same year he proposed to the pope that if the pope acted against anti-Semitism, he would undertake in return to initiate a mass movement for the "free and honourable" conversion of the Jews.[9] "Ant-Semitism," he wrote in 1895, "which is a strong if unconscious force among the masses, will do the Jews no harm."[10] There are moments in *Der Judenstaat* that read as if they had been lifted from an anti-Semitic tract: "When we sink, we become a revolutionary proletariat, the subordinate officers of all revolutionary parties; and at the same time, when we rise, there rises also our terrible power of the purse"; the immediate cause of anti-Semitism is "our excessive production of mediocre intellects."[11]

As has often been pointed out, Herzl was adept at exploiting anti-Semitism; he was unabashed, not to say enthusiastic, in using it as a means of trying to persuade the dignitaries of Central Europe and Turkey of the validity of a Jewish state. A Jewish state would solve the Jewish problem: "I have the solution to the Jewish question," he insisted to Moritz Güdemann.[12] And not just for the Jews. The nations of the world would remove a "foreign body," or political irritant, from their midst: "We will take the Jews away from the revolutionary parties," he argued to the kaiser in 1898.[13] Concerned that his support for the project would be construed as anti-Semitism, the kaiser was reassured—"Further I said," Herzl notes in his diaries after their first meeting in 1896, " 'If your Royal Highness's benevolent attitude toward the Jews became known, your duchy would get such an influx of Jews that it would be highly calamitous.' " (Herzl also argued that his plan would "drain off the surplus Jewish proletariat.")[14] "The anti-Semites will become our most dependable friends, the anti-Semitic countries our allies."[15] When the kaiser met the sultan as part of his failed attempt, orchestrated by Herzl, to persuade the Ottoman ruler to allow the Jews into Palestine, the kaiser is purported to have said: "The Jews are a plague everywhere. We want to get rid of them."[16] It was of course futile. To a similar approach by Herzl several years before, the sultan had replied that he could not relinquish "any part of it" for it belongs "not to me but to the Turkish people."[17]

In fact Herzl provides a far more complex analysis of anti-Semitism than these moments suggest. Anti-Semitism, he suggests in *Der Judenstaat*, is the result of emancipation—"our enfranchisement came too late" (in his diaries he elaborates, "The emancipation of the Jews, which I consider just as much a failure on political grounds as I support it enthusiastically and gratefully for human reasons, came too late").[18] Being a German is therefore cause of anti-Semitism, not cure. The Jews are the exception to Enlightenment. Ahad Ha'am made exactly the same point: "The general rule of progress holds good; but, like other rules, it has its exception, and the exception is the Jewish question."[19] It was folly, he insisted in "Progress and Anti-Semitism," to believe that anti-Semitism would eventually be seen as a mere "error of logic," in contradiction to the progressive spirit of the age—folly to imagine that "the shadows would vanish immediately and the sun of emancipation would shine on the Jews."[20] In his autobiography, Weizmann pours scorn on his schoolteacher's conviction that "a little enlightenment, judiciously applied, and anti-Semitism would simply vanish." In the end, hearing his schoolmaster proclaim "for the 100th time, that if the Germans could only have their eyes opened to the excellent qualities of the Jews, etc., I answered desperately, 'Herr Doktor, if a man has a piece of something in his eye, he doesn't want to know if it is a piece of mud or a piece of gold. He just wants to get it out'."[21]

As Hannah Arendt pointed out, emancipation, while pretending to give the Jew equality, in fact makes the Jew stand out more visibly, as pure difference, from the rest. Surrounded by enemies or released into seeming freedom, the Jew is perennially in the wrong place. The problem in understanding anti-Semitism, Herzl insists to music and literary critic Ludwig Spiegel, his colleague on the *Neue Freie Presse*, is a lack of historical analysis: "The peoples about us who lack an historical understanding—in a word, all of them—do not see us as the historical product of cruelty."[22]

Herzl did not therefore become a Zionist suddenly and in response to the Dreyfus affair of 1894, as is often claimed, even if Dreyfus was key, the moment when belief in a just world for Jews in Europe started to collapse. "We all believed," writes Ahad Ha'am in "Progress and Anti-Semitism," "that elementary justice had become an integral part of European life. Now we see that we were wrong."[23] (Hans Kohn, on the other hand, saw the protest of the intellectuals against the Jewish officer's conviction for treason as proof of "the alert and enlightening conscience against the suggestiveness of national faith.")[24] For Herzl, Dreyfus, together with the mounting Jew-hatred of the Hapsburg Empire, leads to a theory of Jewish identity in its agonistic mode.[25] Jewish identity is forged not internally—this would be anathema to the Orthodox and indeed to Ahad Ha'am—but from the outside: "We are one people. Our enemies have made us one *in our despite*."[26] Hence the need for a Jewish state.

In comments like these, Herzl is laying down a line that will become central not just to Zionism but to the whole future of the Israeli nation, the line that runs from suffering to political power (Herzl's was precisely *political*, not *cultural*, Zionism). A Jewish state had become a right, as only a few years previously Heinrich Graetz, the great Jewish historian, claimed the freedom of the Jews in the civilized world had become a right, "*acquired through thousandfold suffering.*"[27] Jews are "the historical products of cruelty."

Demanding historical understanding—which, note, all people lack—Herzl has made cruelty something like the raison d'être of the Jew. Roughly a quarter of a century later in 1922, faced with a renewed bout of attacks on European Jews, the Zionist organisation will claim, "We owe it to ourselves to be cruel." They continue, "Let us once master the situation and we will be able to say: let the massacres happen, but we, we save the Yishuv before all else, we uphold its future because today it is in the Yishuv, and only there, that the destiny of our people is alive."[28] In these words, in the passage from atrocity to destiny to empowerment, Georges Bensoussan comments, we effectively witness the coming into being of the state. Only the Yishuv. "Resisting fate is not enough," Ben-Gurion states in "Imperatives of the Jewish Revolution," a speech he delivered in Haifa in 1944. "Not non-surrender to the *Galut* [exile] but making an end of it."[29] Responding to the threat to European Jewry, Ben-Gurion repeats a fundamental Zionist belief. Only in Palestine do the Jews have a future. Only with the founding of the state can the history of the Jews be redeemed. "It is the natural right of the Jewish people, like any other people," declares the 1948 Declaration of Independence, "to control their own destiny in their sovereign State."[30] All the other Jews of the world disappear from view. Israel alone counts.

In the 1890s, when Herzl was writing, and 1922, when the Zionist organization made its remark, atrocity against the Jews of Europe had of course barely begun, at least compared with what was to follow. But no discussion of Zionism can make sense if it does not start by acknowledging both the reality of historical anti-Semitism and the effect of persecution against Jews on what I want to call the political Zionist mind. So often in discussion of Zionism we seem to be faced with a false alternative: acknowledge that suffering *or* castigate the injustice of the Israeli state (the charge that any critique of Israel is anti-Semitic merely rides on the back of this false choice). When Edward Said wrote his 1997 piece "Bases for Coexistence" arguing that acknowledgment of Jewish suffering was not antagonistic to, but the means for, coexistence between the two peoples, he received his first hate mail in the Arab press.[31]

What people—a people—make of their suffering is of course the key. It is part of my argument in this chapter that when suffering becomes an identity, it has to turn cruel in order to be able to bear, or live with, itself (the cruel ironies of history take on another sense). Responding in July 2003 to questions about the killing of children by the Israeli army—in the present conflict, one in five dead Palestinians is a child—the commander in Gaza commented, "Every name of a child here, it makes me feel bad because it's the fault of my soldiers." But by the end of the conversation, he has—in the words of his interviewer—returned to being "combative": "I remember the Holocaust. We have a choice, to fight the terrorists or to face being consumed by the flames again."[32] How—the question of this final chapter—did one of the most persecuted peoples of the world come to embody some of the worst cruelties of the modern nation-state?

There is a strange moment in Herzl's *Altneuland* that might help us to focus this question. Kingscourt is trying to persuade Friedrich to visit Palestine. Berating the Jews for lacking a sense of honor, "or they wouldn't sit still under all we're doing to them," he tells the story of a young Jewish boy who broke his arm when he jumped his horse in defiance of Kingscourt, who had taunted him during a visit to his riding school—"You'd rather fly kites than ride hosses." "I had more respect for him." "Because he broke his arm?' "No . . . but because he showed he had a strong will inside that puny body."[33] His fall is an omen. It is as if the future of the new Jewish nation rests on the frail but indomitable strength of that young Jewish boy (the future president of the new nation is David Litwak, whom Friedrich first meets and befriends as a poverty-stricken child in Vienna). As if Herzl also knew, although he always denied it, that Jewish nationalism contained a violence that would have to find somewhere to go. While the moral of this tale may at one level be obvious—strong will, weak body, a will to power rising up against the historic disempowerment of the Jews—it is nonetheless worth noting that it is the Jew's body that has to break. Today, as a matter of policy, the Israeli army breaks the bones of the Palestinians. At the outbreak of the first intifada, Rabin issued an order to the army: "Break their bones."[34] We also have the testimony of soldiers such as Yossi Safed: "The soldiers obediently carried out the orders they had been given: to break the arms and legs by clubbing the Arabs";[35] as well as the footage included in John Pilger's film *Palestine Is Still the Issue*, screened on Carlton Television in England in September 2002. How did we get from there to here?

The word "Zionist" was coined in 1890 by Nathan Birnbaum, founding editor of the first German Jewish-nationalist journal, *Selbst-Emanzipation* (*Self-Emancipation*), in Vienna in 1885. "Zionist" first appeared in the pages of the journal as a substitute for the customary formula "Jewish nationalist," before finding its way into the journal's title, which became *Self-Emancipation: Organ of the Zionists* in 1893. (Disaffected with Herzl, Birnbaum finally drifted into the orthodox anti-Zionist movement, Agudat Israel, founded in Poland in 1912.) That the word "Zionist" is born out of a journal entitled *Self-Emancipation* is telling. Pinsker's pamphlet of the same name, *AutoEmancipation!*, had appeared in 1882. The destiny of the Jews is their task alone. "The meaning of the Jewish revolution," Ben-Gurion states in 1944, "is contained in one word—independence. . . . *We must master our fate; we must take our destiny into our own hands!*"[36] Jewish selfhood comes into being by its own hand. "One of the greatest wonders in their wondrous history," he repeats in the preface to his memoir, is the renewed belief of the Jews in their "own ability . . . to take their fate into their own hands."[37]

And yet, only a few pages later, Ben-Gurion presents the "supreme secret of being," understood only by the prophets, as Job's abjection before God. When Job challenges God, he replies, "Where wast thou when I laid the foundations of the earth?" "And Job submissively acknowledges," Ben-Gurion continues, " 'I know thou canst do everything and that no purpose can be withholden from Thee.' "[38] Job also says, although these lines are not quoted, "Behold I am vile. . . . I abhor myself and repent in dust and ashes."[39]

From abjection to omnipotence, Ben-Gurion does not quite, although I think we should, make the link. On March 20, 1948, when U.S. senator Warren B. Austin announces, to Zionist consternation, that his government will propose to the UN an internal trusteeship over Palestine, Ben-Gurion responds: "We are masters of our own fate. We have laid the foundations for the establishment of a Jewish State *and we will establish it.*"[40] Because it always knew somewhere that what it was doing was not feasible, Zionism also knew—indeed proclaims—that it would, if need be, defy the will of the world, be not just forceful but omnipotent.

It was the horrors of the Second World War that gave to the Jewish people an unanswerable case—the UN commissioners of 1947 who recommended partition of Palestine did so after visiting the displaced persons camps of Europe: "the visible horrors of the Holocaust," writes Ilan Pappe, "would do much to reduce UNSCOP's choice (the United Nations Special Committee on Palestine) when it came to decide on the question of Palestine."[41] The connection has some unlikely adherents. At a London screening of his controversial film, *Jenin, Jenin*, filmed in spring 2002 during the Israeli siege of Jenin in the West Bank, the director, Palestinian-Israeli filmmaker and actor Mohammed Bakri, was asked by a journalist in the audience, "Can you tell me what reason there is for the State of Israel?" to which he replied, "The Holocaust."[42]

What I am describing does not, however, start with the Holocaust. This is Chaim Weizmann in 1919: "I do not think all the opposition in the world will stop us." "It will become Zion whether the Sultan wants it, or anybody else wants it." "What did we say to the British statesmen? We told them 'The Jews will get to Palestine anyhow, whether you want it or not. There is no power on earth that can stop the Jews from getting to Palestine.' "[43] Physically Zionism wrenches its destiny out of the earth: "We think that you possess a thing only when you build it with your own hands."[44]

As we saw in chapter 1, the restitution of Israel was for many Zionists a divinely appointed task (for the Orthodox opponents of Zionism this was the sacrilege). But the ethos of the first Zionist pioneers can also be seen as an act of usurpation lifted, in detail, straight out of God's words to Job: "Who hath divided a watercourse for the overflowing of waters? . . . To cause it to rain on the earth where no man is; on the wilderness where there is no man. To satisfy the desolate and waste ground; and to cause the bud of the tender herb to spring forth? . . . Hast thou an arm like God?"[45] Remember Rabbi Alkalai in 1843: "[O]ur land is waste and desolate, and we shall have to build houses, dig wells, and plant vines and olive trees."[46] Water will be politically crucial, a repeated stumbling block to peace—the Palestinian Authority has never been granted control of the water supplies. Today the settlements in the West Bank have seven times, and those in Gaza fourteen times the water supply of the Palestinians in refugee camps. If the wall keeps to its current lines, Israel will have effectively confiscated 50 percent of the water supply from the new Palestinian state. "I hope," Weizmann states to the Zionist Congress in London in 1919, "that the Jewish frontiers of Palestine will be as great as Jewish energy for getting Palestine. We must get all the waters which belong to Palestine to flow into Palestine."[47] In 1920, the International Union of Labor Zionists presented a memorandum to the British Labour Party, prepared by Ben-Gurion: "It is necessary that the water sources, upon which the future of the Land depends, should not be outside the borders of the future Jewish homeland."[48]

The claim of the Jews to the land—tenuous historically, all the more ruthlessly claimed biblically—rests therefore on the unique quality of Jewish self-fashioning, its ability to carve fate into the soil. Only this can justify the dispossession of the Arabs: "The development of Palestine could not be held up by squatters who did nothing except superficially scratch it . . . it was the service to the soil which determined the right in our favour"; "The Jewish population of Palestine has grown to about 600,000 and it is inconceivable that this Community which is dynamic, active, conscious of its strength, can be dominated by something like a million backward Arabs." "If we settle 50,000 families on the land in Palestine, it will be Jewish, whether the Arabs want it or not."[49]

It is therefore an error, I think, to believe that political Zionism was ever naive or blind or innocent. That it was not aware, from very early on, both of the miraculous dimension of its own ambitions and of the likely cost.

That this cost was internal, and recognized only too clearly by some, was the point of the previous chapter. Here, we are looking at the political repercussions on the ground, at who paid the price. But whereas it is often argued that protest on behalf of the Palestinians should take precedence over lament for the state of Israel's soul, I would suggest that this is a false distinction. The two are, and have always been, indissoluble. Not just in the profound connections between these two Semitic peoples—"they are," wrote Weizmann in 1940, "to some extent our cousins";[50] nor in the unavoidably and catastrophically shared history; nor in the often denied economic dependency of Israel on the Palestinians who provide its essential casual labor supply; nor—more optimistically—in the renewed call for a binational or postnational state. All of these are crucial, but there is something else. It is my belief that Zionism could not have perpetrated its injustice toward the Arabs were it not for the violence that even its most fervent political advocates always knew it was doing, not only to the Arabs, but to itself.

Confronted with the opposition of large sections of British Jewry to the Zionist project, Weizmann's address to the British Zionist Federation in 1919 reaches a pitch of urgency and what I think can only be described as frenzy:

> What did it mean? . . . What did we ask? . . . I repeat it again. By a Jewish national home I mean the creation of such conditions that as the country is developed we can . . . finally establish such a society in Palestine that Palestine

> shall be as Jewish as England is English, or America American. . . . Is it to be a Jewish state in the future or not? (cries of "Yes")[51]

To survive, or defy, its own internal contradictions, Zionism has to get carried away with itself.

Zionism was not meant of course to be a military endeavor. It was not meant to be violent. It was not meant to be the bearer of injustice toward an indigenous people. But we can perhaps trace the beginnings of what was to come to the start of the century when, in the face of the Russian pogroms of 1904 and 1905, Jewish self-defense becomes a reality for the first time at the exact moment that the question of political independence takes shape in the mind of some Russian Jews: "a slow apprenticeship in violence, a turning point, like the first steps of emancipation from traditional education, like liberation from the ancient straitjacket of fear."[52] Violence becomes a form of creativity, a form of "constructive aggression" that then, barely before it has developed into an ethos and precisely because it so goes against the grain, has to surpass itself. In a poem by Yosef Brenner of 1905, a Russian adolescent boy explains to his mother why he is joining a unit for Jewish self-defense: "Hear! O Israel! Not an eye for an eye! Two eyes for one, and all their teeth for any kind of humiliation!" His father, killed during the last pogrom, had not even tried to defend himself.[53]

In fact these earliest stirrings of self-defense were by no means always attached to Zionism—the first such demonstration came in 1903 from the socialist Bund, the group of socialist Jews virulently opposed to Jewish nationalism. But one Russian Jew from Odessa, for whom the link would become unbreakable, was Vladimir (Ze'ev) Jabotinsky, founder of Revisionist Zionism (born in 1880, he was witness to the pogroms). Jabotinsky is most famous for his concept of the "iron wall": in order to thwart Arab resistance to the Jewish colonization of Palestine, the Jews must make themselves unassailable.[54] But long before the Arab riots of the early 1920s crystallized this concept in his mind, Jabotinsky believed that combat was the only path of survival for the Jews. When I asked Benjamin Netanyahu about Jabotinsky's iron wall in 2002, he commented: "The iron wall was not merely the fence. The iron wall was the idea of deterrence, to have them smash against your defenses or against your offenses" (at the word "smash," he punched his fist).[55] Netanyahu is right—Jabotinsky's wall was never meant to take on the brute concretization of the fence being built in Israel today. "For Jabotinsky the iron wall was a metaphor," Avi Shlaim, whose study of Israel is called *The Iron Wall*, commented recently; "in the crude hands of Ariel Sharon and his colleagues, this metaphor is being metamorphosed into a monstrous physical reality."[56] It was also meant to be a first stage leading to negotiations, whereas today "the danger to Israel is to fall in love with the iron wall and refuse to move to Stage II."[57]

Nonetheless, it was because Jabotinsky's vision was so unflinching that—like the writers considered in the previous chapter but from a diametrically opposed politics—he often spoke the truth. These lines, from the speech he delivered to the socialist youth movement in Warsaw on July 12, 1938, are worth quoting:

> This youth truly believed their ideal of peace could be fulfilled. They believed in fraternity with the Arabs. They hoped they would never have to pick up a gun. They hoped to establish a "communal syndicate," just as they believed in the ideal of worker unity without racial or national distinctions. They figured that workers of all nations would stretch out to them in order to fulfill these ideals of peace and fraternity. So they hated their guns and were repulsed by all weapons. They swore they would never touch one. . . . Of course, such a vision was illusory and contemptible, but nonetheless it contained principles, an ideal, and a hope. So dear enemies, what has been your destiny? What has become of your principles, hopes, and ideals? You march rifle in hand; you have turned into soldiers, you conjure up a great army, boast of your heroic exploits, and already even your children like playing at war, each one proud of having "felled ever so many Arabs."[58]

The analysis, as Bensoussan comments, is pitiless. Compare these words from the exhibition that opened in July 2004 on Hebron: "Once a little kid, a boy of about six, passed by me at my post," writes one of the soldiers who had served there. "He said to me, 'Soldier, listen, don't get annoyed, don't try and stop me, I'm going out to kill some Arabs.' "[59] "Of all the necessities of national rebirth," Jabotinsky stated in 1947, "shooting is the most important of all."[60] Like, or rather unlike, Buber, Kohn, and Arendt, Jabotinsky knew that violence would be the destiny of a Jewish state.

It is, however, former prime minister, present finance minister (and prime minister-in-waiting) Benjamin Netanyahu—whose allegiance to Jabotinsky we have already seen—who turns apology into identity. "With the founding of the State of Israel," he writes in 1993 in *A Place among Nations: Israel and the World*, "in the space of only a few years a reborn Jewish sovereignty rediscovered the art of soldiering."[61] It is not to be lamented—far from it—that the nation turns all its citizens into soldiers. For Netanyahu, in order to survive, Jewishness must incorporate its own repudiated violence: "No nation in the world will choose to ally itself with Israel because it has returned to parading the virtue of Jewish powerlessness"—the chapter from which these quotations are taken is entitled "The Question of Jewish Power."[62] That power must be military before anything else: "for the Jews even reimplanting an understanding of the elementary need for *military* power entailed a bitter battle to overcome the entrenched view that Jews ought to have nothing to do with armies."[63] On Israel today: "The escapist tendencies of Jewish politics stem from this Jewish inability to reconcile oneself to the permanent need for Jewish power"—note *Jewish* (not *Israeli*) politics, *Jewish* (not *Israeli*) power.[64]

For Buber, Kohn, and Arendt, the incipient militarism of the new state was a trap, the consequence of its injustice toward the indigenous peoples. In Netanyahu's thinking, it appears more as an internal matter, "a millennial question" that forms part of Jewishness's spiritual and historical reckoning with itself; where he does discuss the Arab claim to the land, it is dismissed (that Arabs are terrorists and that the world must mobilize against terror, to which end he founded the Jonathan Institute in Washington in the 1970s, is the reverse side of the same coin).[65] Buber, Arendt, and Kohn would agree that there is something inside the ethos of Judaism that runs counter to the militarization of nationhood. But for them, that ethos should act as a brake on power; for Netanyahu, it is the regrettable consequence of the Diaspora, which triggered this "long, horrible transformation of the Jews."[66]

With disarming clarity—otherwise he would not be worth quoting—Netanyahu urges on the Jewish people the need to foster an identification with the most lethal components of statehood *as the answer to their own history.* It was the historic task of Zionism, specifically of Herzl and Jabotinsky, to empower the Jews, against all those critics who warned that the "establishment of Jewish military might would throw the Jews into the arms of militarism and extreme nationalism." Israel takes its place "among nations" (the book's title).[67] Today, writes David Grossman in 2002, in something close to despair over Israel's future, "Israel is more militant, nationalist and racist than it has ever been before."[68] Two years after the outbreak of the second intifada, any alternative vision is finding it harder and harder to gain a hearing. Sharon's cunning has been to make it seem that "the only answer to the complicated question: 'How does Israel make itself secure?' is 'By force.' That is the field of Sharon's expertise. Force, more force and only force."[69] The question is complicated. Brute force is not the best answer to real fear.

Sharon does not speak for all Israelis, as Grossman's voice attests, although his military policies receive widespread assent (no critique of the army's actions in Rafah was expressed at the peace demonstration in May 2004). Nor has his obdurate refusal to negotiate with the Palestinians been the only path that Israel, in the past decades, has tried to pursue. Nevertheless Sharon has commanded massive support, precisely—in Grossman's analysis—for his brute, physical, embodiment of strength. The question then must be asked: is Sharon an aberration or does he represent Israel's dark night of the soul? Is he a travesty, or rather does he, by giving flesh to an abiding logic of Zionist thought, bring to fruition the nation's most powerful, unanswerable, vision of itself?

What, we might ask, are you meant to do with suffering? More pertinent still, in the case of Jewish history, what are you meant to do with fear? Zionism arises on the back of European anti-Semitism, on the one hand, and the pogroms of Eastern Europe on the other. As well as being fueled by the birth of nineteenth-century nationalism, the drive to Jewish self-determination must be understood as the response to that history. But the question still remains of what happens to fear when it entrenches itself inside a political identity and life. One of the things this history shows is how fear becomes unanswerable, a sacred object that hardens like a crystal in the soul. To even raise the question of where it travels inside the life of a people can then appear as sacrilege.

But we only have to look to the early Zionists for a warning of the dangers of fear. Yosef Brenner, who would be witness to the murder of his sister in the Russian pogroms of 1905, makes this plea in 1904:

> How can they go on living as if nothing was happening? Will they be able to wipe from their memories the rape and torture of their sisters, the massacres of their children and their mothers . . . ? Will they be able to forget the iron blow that kills, the hellish tumult of the pogroms? I feel my spirit tremble, my brother. . . . My spirit trembles and grows dark. . . . My spirit fails and my hands grow weak. Will you tell me that, in times of crisis, hands must not weaken? Perhaps, but what will strong hands do? I ask you: what path will be chosen by hands that are strong?[70]

In 1918, after the Balfour Declaration, A. D. Gordon asks: "What are we looking for in the land of Israel? Isn't it basically to be what peoples are today and which important forces among them are pleading to be no longer: a predatory people with a threatening fist."[71]

You can track the path from the Russian self-defense units; to HaShomer, the militia of young Zionists constituted in Palestine between 1907 and 1914 to protect the new agricultural settlements; to the Jewish battalions that fought alongside the British army in 1917–1918; to the creation of the Haganah, the kernel of the modern Jewish army created clandestinely in 1920, and the Palmach, its crack fighting force, formed—as historian Tom Segev points out—in full cooperation with the British and under their sponsorship.[72] The Irgun's final inclusion in the Israeli Defense Forces in 1948, after major difficulty that caused Buber such concern, would simply be the next stage.[73] The recourse to arms that Gordon fears is, for a contemporary like Berl Katznelson, the national spirit in the making: "the road that history has chosen to test the strength and enthusiasm of the people."[74]

Above all, something shifts between the first waves of immigrants into Palestine and their children, a conflict of fathers and sons. For the new generation, the Arab revolts of 1936–39 will be decisive. The figure of the warrior replaces that of the pioneer. The father has to be taught by his child: "Father, life in this country requires the revolver, the knife, the bomb, murder, like everywhere else."[75] Why, he asks—a question often put in discussions of Israel and Zionism—should the Jewish nation be different from, better than, the rest?

Trapped between the founders of the homeland and the immigrants who will flood in after the war, this generation, although it will be decisive, is oddly suspended in time and finds its only place of maneuver in the world of military power. Out of its ranks will come Moshe Dayan, Shimon Peres, and Itzhak Rabin. "We did not have to live in the midst of pogroms to experience their social effects, or to know that the gentile world was poisoned," writes Weizmann in his autobiography. "The acquisition of knowledge was not so much a normal process of education as the *storing up of weapons* in an arsenal by means of which we hoped later to be able to hold our own in a hostile world."[76] From the pogroms to Balfour to today, Brenner's question resounds: "what will strong hands do?"

Zionism therefore gives us the unique opportunity to watch the militarization of suffering, to watch suffering become at one and the same time silenced and *its own cause*. "You will never arouse in Jewry a movement in favour of a general territory," writes Mirkin, colleague of Nahman Syrkin, in 1903, "but only for a specifically Palestinian"—only for that territory will Jews be willing to suffer.[77] As early as 1881, in response to a wave of pogroms, Moshe Lilienblum wrote in his diary of May 7: "*I am glad I have suffered*. The rioters approached the house I am staying in. The women shrieked and wailed, hugging the children to their breasts, and didn't know where to turn. The men stood by dumbfounded. We all imagined that in a few moments it would all be over with us . . . but thank God they were frightened away by the soldiers and we were not harmed. *I am glad I have suffered*."[78] The founding of the nation—many of the early Zionists of course came to Palestine in direct flight from the Russian pogroms—then becomes, not so much restitution, as a colossal *sublimation* of historical pain: "The dreadful unity of our sufferings, our protestations, our moans and cries, everything stifled in our throats that fear of the enemy prevents us from externalizing, we must for now sublimate in the gigantic work we are undertaking for the saving and resurrection of our people" (Yosef Vitkin launching his influential appeal to Russian youth in 1905).[79]

Inside this logic there is another deadly twist. Suffering, not just the response to real and present danger, becomes something like a national disgrace. Once the link was made between suffering and humiliation, once—we might say—the problem of historical injustice became a narcissistic wound, then any perceived assault on the Jews, regardless of its reasons, becomes, not just a danger (and even when in fact no danger at all), an affront to the Jewish self. The history of the creation of the Israeli nation is in part the history of one displacement after another, in which, time and time again, the enemies of the Jews turn into the shades of past persecution, each one at once real and unreal, infinitely dangerous and a ghost. For the first *olim*, barely armed Arab marauders against early Jewish settlement took on the features of mass city rioters buttressed, if not incited, by the full apparatus of the Russian state.

Arab rights can be dismissed; the Arab people—only too visible—can or rather must be defeated, because any concession is repetition. Weakness always excites hate. The Arab is a worthless primitive: "We should not forget that we are dealing with a semi-savage people with extremely primitive concepts. This is their nature: if they sense that you are strong, they will yield to you and repress their hatred; if they sense that you are weak, they will dominate you"—the words in 1913 of Labor Zionist Moshe Smilansky, who had in fact written extensively against the coercion of the Arabs.[80] Or as Jabotinsky puts it in 1939, "Whoever is not afraid of biting with all his 32 teeth is accepted as a partner."[81] In May 2003, Jonathan Spyer, former adviser to the current Likud government on international relations, wrote to the *Guardian* newspaper: "Israeli submission would invite further aggression. . . . When we seem weak, we are attacked."[82] "As soon as the Jewish people start to walk with its head held high, upright," states Chana Bart of Kfar Darom in June 2004, one of sixty-five families facing evacuation under Sharon's plan, "the Arabs will lower their heads, and the situation will work out."[83] According to this logic, every achievement of the Palestinians in negotiations is perceived as a crushing internal defeat (Yasser Arafat's return to Gaza after the Oslo Accord became a national humiliation).[84]

Go back to Smilansky's comment, and its orientalism—"a semi-savage people with extremely primitive concepts"—almost appears as a form of reluctant memory, a thinly veiled form of self-contempt. It is because the Jew has been so shamed in history that his enemy today is at once so dangerous and so cheap. After all, one of the charges against the Jews was that they, too, engaged in primitive rites: "We consider ourselves fortunate,' writes Lilienblum in 1884, "when an enlightened, well-meaning Christian testifies that human blood is not in fact part of our menu at Easter. Under such affronts, thus shamefully, are we willing to live."[85]

At times, reading this history is like watching a dog chasing its own tail. Arab aggression is not provoked by Jewish settlement of the land; it is not a response to dispossession. It is a challenge to the Jewish people not to capitulate to their own past. "The fate of a nation," writes historian J. L. Talmon, lecturer at the Hebrew University of Jerusalem, in 1957, "like that of a person, may be the working out of traumas of early childhood, in short the outcome of some basic decisive experience. . . . The refusal of the Arab states to recognise Israel looks like a counterpoint of the Western-Christian treatment of Jews as latecomers and aliens."[86] Once you trace this sequence, then the apparently extreme vision of Kach's Rabbi Kahane takes up its historical place: "A fist in the face of an astonished gentile world that had not seen it for two millennia," he wrote in 1976 in response to a terrorist attack on a settlement, "this is Kidush Hashem [sancification of the name of God]."[87] Faced with pronouncements such as this, we might fairly ask: who exactly do the Arabs represent?

It is, then, one of the tragedies of this conflict that the Palestinians have become the inadvertent objects of a struggle that, while grounded in the possession of the land, at another level has nothing to do with them at all. A struggle that makes of them the symbolic substitutes, stand-ins, "fall guys," we could almost say, for something no longer spoken out loud, something quite else. "The Palestinians . . . have arisen to destroy us," writes Udi Buch in a letter to *Ha'aretz* in October 2004.[88] I have become convinced that in political conflicts of any obduracy, nobody is ever playing only the part of himself. It goes without saying of course—although this, too, is often a consequence of such primordial, enduring, mostly unspoken displacements—that nobody is ever in the right place.

In the context of Zionism, once the equation was set, once suffering had become degradation, any ethical sensitivity toward the indigenous people was viewed with abject horror, a form of self-indicting passivity, historical repetition, the Jews once again enslaved to fear. The Diaspora Jew is a wretch. To redeem him, or rather have done with him, the usage of force in Palestine becomes a gift. And the moral mission of Israel promoted by Buber, and by those who supported him—the claim that Israel should be a nation not like, but unlike, to all others—becomes a failure of nerve. Enough of "Jewish hyper-moralism," Ze'ev Smilansky writes in 1908; he was responding to Itzhak Epstein, who the year before in Ahad Ha'am's journal *HaShiloah* had argued that the Jewish nation must not be built without respect for morality and justice, the essential foundations of Zionism (his article was not well received).[89] Once again it is Jabotinsky who spells it out most clearly: "A nation without a homeland must remain eternally without a homeland. The world has been divided up and so it must be. That is morality for you."[90] Or to put it more simply: Do you want ethics or do you want land?[91]

Today we can see this argument reach its logical conclusion in the claim that any criticism of Israel is anti-Semitic because it makes an unfair ethical demand on the Jew. "By negating Zionism," writes Emanuele Ottolenghi in his article "Anti-Zionism Is Anti-semitism," "the anti-semite is arguing that the Jew must always be the victim, for victims do no wrong."[92] As if ethics, even fear for the Jewish people, might not be at the root of anxiety about the direction the country is taking: "What is happening in Israel," states retired army general Avner Azulay, director of the Rich Foundation in Tel Aviv, "is bad for the Jewish people in the long term. It seems to be coming true that what is happening in Israel is damaging for Jews."[93] As if hatred were always the foundation, and the only foundation, of critique. "Who is the true friend of Israel," asks Daniel Ben-Simon, "the loving critic or the unthinking patriot?"—or, in the words of Gideon Levy, famous campaigning journalist on behalf of Palestinians, also of *Ha'aretz*, "Is the true friend of Israel one who identifies with it automatically, or one who wants it to be just?"[94]

"Many good people who feel no hatred towards the Jews but who detest the persecution of the Palestinians," Uri Avnery writes, "are now called anti-Semites."[95] Instead one might argue, as Arendt for example argued, that seeing the Jews' predicament as expressive of eternal anti-Semitism, rather than as part and parcel of the political realities of the modern world, was, and continues to be, one of political Zionism's most fundamental mistakes. "My son Arik was not murdered because he was Jewish," writes Yitzak Frankenthal, whose son was killed during an attack by Palestinian fighters, "but because he is part of a nation that occupies the territory of another. I know that these are concepts that are unpalatable, but I must voice them loud and clear because they come from the heart—the heart of a father whose son did not get to live because his people were blinded with power."[96]

In 1943, Ernest Simon—former member of Brit Shalom—was invited to address the youth of Kibbutz Gvat in Galilee. Dismayed by the hostility of his young audience, to whom he was attempting to explain the wrongs being perpetrated against the Arabs and his opposition to transfer, he warned, "We are approaching the limit beyond which defence changes from a necessary evil into a complete ideology."[97] He was speaking a year after the Biltmore Declaration of May 1942, when an extraordinary meeting of the American Zionists, attended by both Weizmann and Ben-Gurion, adopted a resolution laying claim to the whole of mandatory Palestine (a subsequent resolution in Atlantic City, confirmed by the World Zionist Organization, made no reference to the Arabs whatsoever).

The young kibbutzniks of Galilee were in tune with the emerging nation. On December 30, 1947, Ben-Gurion addressed the Central Committee of the Histadrut (the syndicate of Labor Zionism): "There can be no stable and strong Jewish state so long as it has a Jewish majority of only 60 percent. . . . We must think like a state."[98] On March 10, 1948, the Haganah High Command put forward the "aggressive defence strategy" *Tochnit Dalet*, or Plan D, which provided for, along with the destruction of whole Arab villages, the expulsion beyond the borders of the new state of any Arab who resisted the Jewish advance; not, as Nur Masalha allows in his crucial study *Expulsion of the Palestinians*, a blueprint for transfer, but nonetheless bearing the imprint of Ben-Gurion who, according to his biographer Michael Bar-Zohar, made clear in internal discussions and instructions that it would be better if "as few as possible of Arabs would remain in the territory of the [Jewish] state."[99] It was, writes Baruch Kimmerling of the Hebrew University of Jerusalem, "a complete demographic, ethnic, social and political transformation of Palestine from an Arab land to a Jewish state."[100] Eight hundred thousand Arabs fled or were expelled. "We are masters of our own fate. We have laid the foundations for the establishment of a Jewish state and we will establish it." "It will be Jewish whether the Arabs want it or not."

Today, the worst details of what happened are only now and very slowly coming to light.[101] Those on the right, as Avi Shlaim has pointed out, are oddly more receptive to this new emerging history than is liberal opinion in Israel, since they consider that the expulsion should have gone further and was fully justified by Arab aggression against the new state (although in an interview before his 2001 election, Sharon stated that the new historians should not be taught). Today inside Israel "transfer" of the Palestinians is once again being openly discussed. And even in the Geneva Agreement, the only peace initiative with the Palestinians currently available, no responsibility is taken by Israel for what happened to the refugees in 1948.

However difficult it is to do so, we must, I believe, understand the place of the Holocaust in the Israeli psyche in this frame. A tragedy, but for the Yishuv, like the pogroms before, also an affront. Something that therefore requires, in response, an act of self-assertion, or *Selbst-Emanzipation*, which—because of the internal humiliation—nothing can, or will, stop (ruthlessness always has an undercurrent of pain). We know that the Holocaust fully enters the national memory only after the 1967 Six-Day War. Only a miracle can wipe out a curse. But that very fact has obscured a reality that seems to me more important. We need to go back further. The fact of something's being unspoken does not mean that it is not silently, but powerfully, at work. "Most painful to me,' writes Sara Roy of her childhood in Israel, "was the denigration of the Holocaust and pre-state Jewish life by many of my Israeli friends. For them, these were times of shame, when Jews were weak and passive, inferior and unworthy, deserving not of our respect but of our disdain."[102]

In Grossman's most famous novel, *See Under: Love*, the nine-year-old Momik has to call up the Nazi beast from the cellar in order to confront his family's silenced European past. Grossman then spins his whole novel—the story of Anshel Wasserman, Momik's survivor grandfather—out of the boy's later, secret, research into the Holocaust. As if the Holocaust were at once a guilty family secret and something that this generation has to invent, or rather reinvent, for itself. Inside the concentration camp that Momik conjures in order to tell Wasserman's story, the Nazi commandant, Neigel, chants like a mantra words Grossman lifts from Hitler's Berlin speech of 1938: "Conscience is the business of the Jews." The narrator comments: "This sentence was interpreted by Jürgen Stroop, the German commander of Warsaw during the rebellion, as follows: 'And thus he freed the Nazis from conscience.' "[103]

Later in the book, the grandfather responds, accepting the burden of Jewish ethical life: "Indeed yes, it is a grave responsibility, and a heavy burden we have never forgotten, never . . . Sometimes we were the last remaining souls on earth who remembered what a conscience is."[104] In a rare moment, the narrator intervenes against his own character, telling us to view these words indulgently, as those of a Jew " 'doomed' to a lifetime of absolute values of morality and conscience," with "no other weapon at hand."[105] Grossman is struggling not to hand the palm to the Nazis—they win, whichever choice you make: reject morality, you become a Nazi; embrace it, they destroy you. In the face of these deadly alternatives, the only option for conscience, like justice, is to relativize—or more crudely to compromise—itself. The narrator continues: "The strong have power, and when power demands to be actualised, it creates complex situations in which sometimes a decision must be made between two flawed, alternative approaches to justice, leading of necessity to relative injustice."[106]

Grossman's is the most subtle version of a link we have already seen, the link between a morality suspected of being abject—later the narrator refers to Wasserman's "passive, righteous attitude,"[107]—and defeat; or to push it one stage further, the felt clash between ethics and a Jewish state. If conscience, no nation. The grandfather's pathos, his too-absolute-morality, would make it impossible for the Jews of the modern world ever to empower themselves. Perhaps it is because he lays out the dilemma so clearly—because he acknowledges the "flaw," not to say injustice, at the heart of the nation—that Grossman has become one of the most vocal critics of the Israeli government of today. "In my Jewish education," writes Carl Sherer to the *Guardian* newspaper from Jerusalem in August 2002, "I was taught that with three exceptions [refraining from idol worship, murder, adultery], the number one Jewish moral imperative is to preserve Jewish lives. Ending Israel's control over another nation was not one of the three exceptions."[108] In this deadly equation, morality toward the Palestinians has become the adversary of the Jewish will to live. "A loud voice keeps shouting," writes first class reservist and refusenik Assaf Oron, "we must put morality and conscience to sleep."[109]

But writers like Grossman and Sara Roy also seem to be saying something else. That it is shame at the Holocaust, not the event, which is a warp on the nation's soul. On the fiftieth anniversary of the liberation of Auschwitz, Grossman writes in the German newspaper *Die Zeit* of the "cruelty" native Israelis had shown toward the survivors, as if both the event and the fact of their survival were causes of "shame."[110] "Call me an antisemite," stated Ben-Gurion less than two weeks before the outbreak of the Second World War, "but . . . we are choking with shame about what is happening. . . . We do not belong to that Jewish people. . . . We do not want to be such Jews."[111] Almost a hundred years before, in 1899, Bernard Lazare had written to Herzl, "[W]e die from *hiding our shames*."[112]

Bringing the Holocaust out of hiding, Grossman speculates in the last part of his novel that perhaps the Jews went to their deaths with such relative ease because they were already so ashamed. Shame, he writes, is like a "sleeping potion" that courses through a people's veins.[113] It is also, this history suggests, the hidden face of pride. Uri Avnery was raised on the heroic myths of Masada and Tel Hai, myths revived and polished with new vigor in Palestine on the eve of the destruction of the European Jews. "They formed the consciousness of the new Hebrew nation."[114] In January 1941, when Germany seemed invincible, an anthology of "Jewish heroism throughout the centuries" was published by the publishing house Am Oved, founded by Berl Katznelson. On March 31, 1942, the journal of the worker's youth movement declares: "The Masada camp will gird us for a life of labour, defence and freedom. *Masada will not fall again*."[115] In the middle of the war, the catastrophe of Masada—a thousand Jews, men, women, and children, committed suicide after a protracted siege by the Romans in C.E. 70—is turned into a triumph.

It is not therefore talking about the Holocaust after 1967 that needs to be examined, but the fact of not—or barely—talking about it before. How could such an act of colossal denial not have the most profound effect on the birth and subsequent evolution of the fledgling nation-state? "Labor Zionism," writes Bensoussan, "had always denigrated Diaspora Jewry but when that same Jewry was wiped out in Europe, Zionism nourished secretly for decades in its breast a guilt that would resurface only in the generation of its grandchildren. Finally the gulf between the Yishuv and the diaspora would be filled, but on the worst possible foundations."[116] Israel, it seems, comes into being on the back of a guilty, repudiated, unconscious identification with its own dead. Dying bodies, visible and invisible, carpet the nation's ground. On the walls of Momik's bedroom hangs a portrait of Prime Minister David Ben-Gurion and a picture of "[v]ultures with their wings spread like steel birds boldly defending our nation's skies."[117]

In the last part of *See Under: Love*, Wasserman, who had been a famous writer, finally tells the story to the commandant that he has been begging him for throughout (all the Nazi wants is to be told stories like a child). The story is of the miracle child Kazik, born to an aging couple; the infant then ages and dies in accelerated time—he is twenty-two hours old when he dies. It is impossible not to read Kazik as an allegory of the Israeli nation. Out of a silence, Grossman charts the death of a nation that has made its whole rationale the will of the Jewish people to survive.

In 2003, two hundred reservists of the Israeli army on duty in Hebron were sent on a visit to Auschwitz to strengthen their military resolve (for good reason—remember Yehuda Shaul, who organized the exhibition of army brutality in Hebron against which he and other soldiers have now turned: "It screws up everyone").[118]

Today, far from being silenced, the Holocaust saturates Israeli consciousness, creating a "one-dimensional identification" between Jewish experience and the Holocaust in the minds of Israeli youth: "Tens of thousands of high school students, on the verge of their enlistment in the army, make pilgrimages to Auschwitz to discover their 'roots'."[119] According to Daniel Ben-Simon, for Limor Livnat, the education minister, "besides the Jews there is nothing else in the world, beside the camp there is nothing else in Europe."[120]

David Zonsheine, the founder of Courage to Refuse, has been nominated for the Nobel Peace Prize by Bishop Belo, the Guatemalan freedom fighter Rigoberta Menchu who was awarded the prize in 1992. Writing of his early stirrings of conscience, he states: "The words that the Shin Bet agent used in the house [of the suspect] were, 'Separate the man from his wife and children.' So the associations with the Holocaust were triggered in me already then, though at the time I had no heretical thoughts. The only associations with the Holocaust at that stage were, that because of everything that happened then, everything that is now happening is fine. They killed us once, and since then we can effectively do whatever we want" (note that completely unallocated "they").[121]

"I remember the Holocaust," stated the commander in Gaza questioned over the deaths of Palestinian children. "We have a choice, to fight the terrorists or to face being consumed by the flames again." This is hallucination, as well as more simply exploitation of the Holocaust to justify the violence of the state. The fear of course is real. There are suicide bombings in which Israeli children have died, rightly condemned not just by many inside Israel, but also by Palestinians, as unacceptable crimes. But the flames on the streets of Tel Aviv and Jerusalem are not the flames of the Holocaust. And whatever the resurgence of anti-Semitism in the world today, which is also only too real, the Holocaust will not happen again. Something is, however, being repeated. For psychoanalysis, things are most likely to repeat themselves when they have been driven underground. During his secret library researches, Momik discovers pictures of a Nazi soldier "forcing an old man to ride another old man like a horse"—"deep down inside he began to sense that these photographs might reveal the first part of the secret everyone had tried to keep from him."[122] "The soldier," writes Sara Roy on the Israeli occupation of Palestine, "ordered the old man to stand behind the donkey and kiss the animal's behind. . . . Throughout the summer of 1985, I saw similar incidents: young Palestinian men being forced by Israeli soldiers to bark like dogs."[123] Today we know, from Abu Ghraib in Iraq to Bagram in Afghanistan, that this is the standard behavior of occupying armies. In the case of Israel, such behavior—of an army that can neither justify nor live with itself—reveals another historical layer, another undercurrent of memory and brutally repudiated pain.

Daily, the evidence suggests, the Israeli army reenacts one of the buried, shameful fragments of the past it most fiercely dreads. In his delusion, the commander in Gaza—and even more his victims—are paying the price of shame. As commentators on both sides of this conflict have often observed, for the Palestinians, humiliation is the worst offense: "the total humiliation which every Palestinian, without distinction of age, gender or social standing, experiences every moment of his life."[124] Not the dispossession, the demolition of homes, the obstruction of daily life, the extrajudicial killings, the destruction of the civilian and political infrastructure, the loss of any sense of a political future—"politicide," to use the term coined by Baruch Kimmerling to describe Sharon's war against the Palestinians. "[Are] the negotiations with the Palestinians," Grossman asks two years after Oslo, "turning into one more stage of humiliation for the Palestinians, into an imposition of surrender for them?" "I have seen the humiliation," Desmond Tutu stated after visiting the occupied territories in 2002. "It reminded me of what happened to us in South Africa, where they . . . took joy in humiliating us."[125]

So do we perish of shame, or rather, as Bernard Lazare suggests in his extraordinary remark, do we die from hiding our shames? Shame swept under the carpet, this history suggests, breeds violence like nothing else. What would it be like to live in a world in which we did not have to be ashamed of shame? When Lazare makes his comment in a letter to Herzl of 1899, he is reproaching Herzl for papering over the cracks. In his rush to create a nation, he is blinding himself to the miserable, impoverished condition of the Eastern European Jew. Herzl wants his people to be perfectly bourgeois, a model nation with finances and government in place: "Like all governments, you want to disguise the truth. . . . You want to be the government of a people that looks 'just so' and your ultimate objective is 'not to display our national shames'." "But," he continues, "I am all for displaying them. . . . We die from hiding our shames, from burying them in deep caves, instead of bringing them out into the pure light of day where the sun can cauterise and purify them. . . . We must educate our nation by showing it what it is."[126]

In May 2003, I was asked to chair the opening of an exhibition organized at the Photographer's Gallery in London showing the work of nine photographers on the Israeli-Palestinian conflict[127]—images that ranged from sheer desolation to the joyous and stubborn persistence of daily life. In the discussion afterward a member of the audience made an equation between the Nazis and Ariel Sharon. I reject the analogy as I did when a student from the organization Friends of Palestine at my University college, Queen Mary—escorting me to chair a meeting to be addressed by refusenik Avi Mayorek—arrived in my office carrying a poster of Sharon with a swastika over his face. There is a difference, I insisted on both occasions, between industrial genocide and ethnic transfer. Such historical distinctions are vital.

But to deny any link between the Holocaust and what is happening in Israel today seems equally misguided for the reasons laid out in this chapter. Even if to grasp this link you have to travel back much further than is normally suggested, to the very beginnings of Zionism. You have to fathom the process whereby people—a people—who have been the object of violence are then faced with the dilemma of what to do with the internal debris of their own past. In an extraordinary moment, Sara Roy describes how her mother and aunt clung to each other weeping when the Russian liberators of their concentration camp gave the survivors free rein to do as they wished with the now captive Germans in their power. All of her writing, and her work in occupied Palestine, Roy herself traces to this moment of repudiated revenge.[128] But it is not revenge that has been at issue here, even if it is a cycle of revenge that so often seems to dominate the landscape of Israel-Palestine. Rather it is the moment when something horrific becomes so psychically intolerable that it has—*at one and the same time*—to be repeated and denied. Nothing that has been said here takes away from the legitimacy of the Jewish people's desire for a homeland, nor from the felt strength of their conviction, however dangerous for the future and unjust toward the indigenous peoples, that they were entitled to build it in Palestine. Even though there were those who, as we saw in the previous chapter, understood that out of the ashes a strange anachronism, against all odds, was being born, at the very moment when Europe was witnessing the catastrophic failure of the modern nation-state. Nations are violent, as they also warned. The sons of the first Jewish fathers are surely right: "Father, life in this country requires the revolver, the knife, the bomb, murder, like everywhere else."[129] But precisely because of the history of the Jewish people, Israel, as it comes into being, gives us an exceptional, magnified vision, of how a wound turns into the cut of a sword, how historically inflicted damage arms itself. "There is a time for men and nations who live by the sword," wrote the Zionist Nietzschean Micah Josef Berdichevski, at the dawn of the last century. "This time is the hour of life in its essential meaning . . . the materialisation of life in its boldest lines."[130]

By 1942, Ben-Gurion and Weizmann had fallen out. Weizmann, Ben-Gurion complained, placed too much trust in the British, while Ben-Gurion, in a move that would be decisive for the destiny of the future nation, was shifting his allegiance toward America. Answering the charge, Weizmann retorts that he has said "no" to many an Englishman, and accuses Ben-Gurion of a "sick imagination"—"the imagination of a man who suffers from sleepless nights and is worried" and who "sees ghosts." He then compares Ben-Gurion's conduct with the purges of Hitler and Mussolini, who bring charges "out of the void": "here are a whole host of imaginary charges to culminate in an act of political assassination." In this welter of accusation and counteraccusation, Weizmann picks out one disagreement as fundamental: "Ben-Gurion has considered for two and a half years that the Army is the single problem of Zionism." "I do not share the view even now," he states, "that Zionism fails or falls on the question of the army." Unlike Ben-Gurion, Weizmann is willing to contemplate failure: "We have failed. We have tried again. We may succeed: we may fail. We may get Palestine without the Army, and we may get the Army and not get Palestine."[131]

There were, as we have already seen, a number of moments when the militarization of Zionism proceeded apace, moments as much of generational as of political crisis in relation to the Arabs where the possibility of coexistence was sacrificed on the altar of a more defensive and then belligerent identity. That the Arabs played their part in rendering such coexistence impossible is not in dispute, although their opposition to the settlement of their land needs, still today, to be understood. It was in the midst of one of these crises, the Arab riots of the early 1920s, that the Histadrut, the organization of Labor Zionism, was brought under the political and financial aegis of the Zionist Organization: "for many,' writes Bensoussan, "the social and the military were thenceforth indivisible."[132] No more amateurism, a strong personality must be appointed to the head of the Zionist executive. In 1921, David Ben-Gurion takes his first step into power at the moment when the social and military projects of the nation-in-waiting join hands.

From that moment on, Israeli identity becomes the identity of the soldier (what Yitzak Laor describes as the nation's "love-affair" with the military begins). "For these male officers," writes Ronit Chacham in his book of interviews with the refuseniks, "being an Israeli citizen and a man meant being a soldier and indicting the Israeli army amounted to questioning an essential part of their identity . . . the army seals the relationship between the citizen and the state."[133] "I'd absorbed all the myths," Yehuda Shaul explains after serving in Hebron, "that the army is the most important thing there is and that you have to take part in it, that the army and security unite everyone. I saw my enlistment as an opportunity to become an Israeli."[134] For Sergeant Assaf Oron, "The daily life of the Palestinians is determined by our belief that everything falls under the rubric of battle."[135]

To read Ben-Gurion's memoir is to be given dramatic insight into how this machinery, or armory, of state takes on the legacy of the messianism discussed in the first chapter, and—fulfilling the worst fears of the voices of the second—starts to roll. In December 1946, Ben-Gurion, as chair of the Zionist executive, is given the special portfolio of defense. Predicting the coming war—"We will be facing the Arabs and this means *not Arab bands but Arab armies*"—he states to a meeting of the Mapai Council in August of the following year, "It is not only a question of our own survival, but the survival of the entire Jewish people, of the enterprise of salvation and deliverance, of the hope and future of all the remnants of the Jews in the world."[136] In fact it is now generally acknowledged that, although the war would be fiercely fought, there was no question in 1948 but that the new State of Israel would survive.

Today, Ben-Gurion concludes, defense "is the *entire doctrine of Zionism*":

> Altogether we purchased 24 airplanes, 59 vessels of various types, 40 tanks, 144 halftracks, 416 artillery pieces, 24 heavy mortars, 158 heavy machine guns, 1417 medium machine guns, 6034 light machine guns, 52,391 rifles, 523 submachine guns, 1755 pistols. We were only able to bring in a small part of this equipment before the establishment of the State. This included 20 airplanes (purchased from the British Army in this country), 52 halftracks, 26 artillery pieces, a heavy machine gun, 54 medium machine guns, 464 light machine guns, 6240 rifles, 417 submachine guns, and 500 pistols.[137]

Ben-Gurion is in the process of creating what he himself repeatedly refers to as an "elite army." "If, nonetheless, we have managed to gain friends [despite the overwhelming oil power of the Arab nations]," he states twenty years later at a special meeting of the Knesset concluding the celebrations for Israel's twentieth Independence Day, "it is solely because of a spiritual superiority." Although, even among a special people, there may be those who are "empty": "this does not detract from the act of being a nation that is chosen and elite . . . *it is only an elite nation that can produce an elite army.*"[138] To paraphrase: we kill better because we are better. The chosenness of the Jewish people passes into tanks, artillery pieces, and machine guns: "Only by developing our moral and intellectual advantage to the maximum will our Army fulfil its objectives of maintaining national security"—(he is citing the first prime minister of Israel submitting the Defense Bill to the Knesset on August 15, 1949).[139] What David Hartman terms the "mystique" of the nation's military capacities becomes a new secular faith.[140] It is a vision that can be traced as far back as 1918, when Shmuel Yavne'eli, leading figure of the Second Aliya and early socialist, proclaimed, "Every person in a Jewish army implements the concept of the Messiah."[141] We have come full circle, or rather made a turn of 180 degrees: from an ethical vision—Buber's, for example—which drew the line at the dispossession of one people by another, to morality as a weapon, a means to an end, the most powerful arm of the modern nation-state.

At a press conference in Paris on November 27, 1967, shortly after the end of the Six-Day War, Charles de Gaulle stated:

> The establishment between the two World Wars . . . of a Zionist Home in Palestine and subsequently, after World War Two, the establishment of the State of Israel aroused many fears at the time. And many people, among them even many Jews, wondered whether the implantation of this

> community on land obtained on more or less justifiable conditions and in the midst of fundamentally hostile Arab nations would not arouse incessant and endless frictions and conflicts. Some even feared that the Jews, hitherto dispersed . . . would after assembling in the place of their ancient greatness transform into burning and conquering ambition the moving hopes that they had expressed for nineteen centuries: "Next year in Jerusalem."[142]

Since Suez, he continues, the world has been confronted with a "warlike Israel bent on expansion."[143] On May 24 he had told foreign secretary Abba Eban that, if Israel was attacked, France would not let the nation be destroyed, but if Israel was the one to attack, "we will denounce your initiative."[144] Although Israel would doubtless be victorious, the situation for many countries in the region would deteriorate, and tension would increase all over the world. "In the final account," he continues, "all these unpleasantnesses will be attributed to you, who will have become conquerors."[145]

Ben-Gurion publishes de Gaulle's statement in full in his memoirs, along with his reply, which, five times as long, amounts to nothing less than a full historical apologia for Israel. Refuting de Gaulle's charges one by one, he produces a narrative in which the creation of the State of Israel is a fulfillment of a messianic expectation, whose every action has been and will be justified, in which "not one Arab was expelled": "The State of Israel that came into being on May 14, 1948, bears no responsibility for the Arab mass flight."[146] Only at rare moments does the cover slip. When, for example, he insists that Israel was free of territorial ambition—"though," he adds, "the entire world, at least the entire Christian and Jewish world [*sic*], considered the land of Israel on both sides of the Jordan one country and hoped it would be restored as promised by the Torah and the Prophets."[147] Or when, in response to the refusal of the European countries, Russia, and the United States to move their embassies to Jerusalem after Israel took over the whole city in 1967, he comments, "I am unaware of a single protest from the United Nations or one of its members when the government of Jordan in 1948 conquered the Old City of Jerusalem and expelled the Jews therefrom."[148] Fleetingly, Ben-Gurion allows that for the "whole world" (which means of course the Christian and Jewish world), Eretz Israel belongs to the Jewish nation by right—he famously refused to define the borders of the new state in 1948. For a moment, he allows expulsion to enter his narrative as the fate, not of course of the Arabs, but of the Jews.

It is a remarkable document by any standards. Not that some of it does not make perfect sense; not that it cannot indeed be read—as Ben-Gurion intends it to be read—as the case for a nation's defense, in the historical, legal, and military meaning of the term. Nonetheless it left me with a problem—glaring for anyone who has tried to follow this tragic history from the birth of Zionism to today. How do you begin to address—we lack the vocabulary—the problem of a political identity whose strength in the world, indeed its ability to survive as an identity, relies on its not being able, or willing, to question itself?

It would be too easy to say that Ben-Gurion is lying, although at moments the cruel disparity between his policies toward the Arabs on the issue of transfer, and what he claims to have been the intention and the course of events, is staggering. Or, if he is lying, then the person he is most fervently trying to convince is himself. Perhaps we should invoke Xeno's famous paradox of the Cretan who says, "I am lying"—the statement, whichever way you compute it, simply abolishes itself (if it is true that he is lying, then he is not a liar; if it is not true that he is lying, then, by his own admission, he is one who speaks the truth). In a famous comment, the psychoanalyst Jacques Lacan claimed to be able to cut this Gordian knot. We can solve it in a stroke, he said, if we simply assume a divided subject, two speaking subjects inside the utterance—one conscious, one unconscious; one who is lying and one who is not. When the commander in Gaza spoke, his utterance split in two—two voices, one compassionate, the other combative, seeming to exist in two different historical moments and on two different psychological planes. Ben-Gurion's narrative, on the other hand, invites dissent because it is too perfect. One could say that he is carrying the weight of a nation rent by its own strength. Nations, as Rebecca West said, in my opening epigraph for this book, can act against their own interests, be at once ferocious and blind. Somewhere, if only unconsciously, Zionism always knew full well what it was doing to itself and to the Palestinians. We must finally build on that. "The day will yet come," wrote Buber in 1949, "when the victorious march of which our people is so proud today, will seem to us like a cruel detour."[149]

The story told here does not get better, resolve, or complete itself. Indeed the structure of the three chapters could be described as counter-Hegelian: vision, critique, violence, they could also have been subtitled thesis, antithesis—but then what? While I was writing them, I approached two distinguished Hegelian philosophers for the term that would be the opposite of "sublation'—Hegel's term for the final absorption of contradiction into a higher stage. We tried "retrogression," "degradation," but neither quite worked. Nor did postmodern critiques of Hegel, which oppose to "sublation" something decentered, disintegrated, or looser, since Israel is not falling apart, or becoming plural and diffused in its identity, but is more and more desperately entrenching itself. Gershom Scholem's 1930 poem "Encounter with Zion and the World" has the minimal and sober subtitle "Decline":

> We were harmed by light of day,
> what grows has need of night.
> We stand in debt to powers
> we never thought to invite.
>
> . . . .
>
> What was within is now without,
> the dream twists into violence,
> and once again we stand outside
> and Zion is without form and sense.[150]

Perhaps "decline" goes some way toward capturing the dismay of those who believed that a Jewish nation could be different, a dismay expressed by Scholem's circle in the 1930s and 1940s, and now by many Jews inside Israel and throughout the world. "What is happening in Israel," states former army general Avner Azulay, "is bad for the Jewish people."[151]

In this study I have tried to trace some of the causes for dismay back to the kernel of the original—wild and urgent—dream. Zionism is more than one thing. But in the ascendant today is a vision of the Jewish nation that is, I believe—precisely because it has, as it so fervently desired, made itself master of its own destiny—in danger of destroying itself.

Notes

Preface

1. Chris McGreal, "Act of Desperation or a Cynical Ploy?" *Guardian*, October 7, 2003.

2. Brian Whitaker, "Zionist Settler Joins Iraqi to Promote Trade," *Guardian*, October 7, 2003.

3. Adam Keller, "Conscientious Objectors—the Worst of Criminals: Report of the Court Session of December 23, 2003," *Ha'aretz*, December 24, 2003, *Gush-Shalom* (Israeli Peace Bloc), www.gush-shalom.org.

4. Monique Chemillier-Gendreau was one of the lawyers representing the Palestinians in the Hague. By hearing the case, the court effectively accepted the Palestinians as a state, as only states are allowed to petition the court (personal communication).

Chapter 1
"The apocalyptic sting": Zionism as Messianism (Vision)

1. Gershom Scholem, *Sabbatai Sevi: The Mystical Messiah 1626–1676* (Tel Aviv: Om Oved), trans. R.J.Z. Werblowsky, Littman Library of Jewish Civilisation (London: Routledge and Kegan Paul, 1973; Princeton: Princeton University Press, 1975), p. 396. The English translation of Scholem uses the spelling Sabbatai Sevi; I have chosen the more common usage—Shabtai Zvi—throughout.

2. Ibid., p. 397.

3. Chaim Weizmann, "The Jewish People and Palestine" (statement before Palestine Royal Commission, Jerusalem, November 25, 1936) (Jerusalem: Office of Zionist Organization, 1936), p. 14.

4. Scholem, *Major Trends in Jewish Mysticism* (1941) (New York: Schocken, 1955), p. 308.

5. Scholem, *Sabbatai Sevi*, p. 691.

6. Ibid.

7. Weizmann, "The Jewish People and Palestine," p. 14.

8. Scholem, *Sabbatai Sevi*, p. 94.

9. Scholem, "Toward an Understanding of the Messianic Idea in Judaism," in *The Messianic Idea in Judaism and Other Essays* (London: Allen and Unwin, 1971), pp. 16–17.

10. Scholem, *Sabbatai Sevi*, p. 347.

11. Ibid., p. 341.

12. Report from Tunis quoted in ibid., pp. 340–41.

13. Ibid., p. 340.

14. Ibid., pp. 348, 246.

15. Ibid., p. 9.

16. Ibid.

17. Ibid., p. 66; Scholem, "Toward an Understanding of the Messianic Idea," p. 6.

18. *Dangerous Liaison: Israel and America*, directed by Nick Read, produced by George Carey and Eamon Matthews, written and presented by Jacqueline Rose (Channel 4 Television, August 24, 2002), transcript of interview with Aaron and Tamara Deutsch, p. 31.

19. Georges Bensoussan, *Une histoire intellectuelle et politique du sionisme 1860–1940* (Paris: Fayard, 2002), p. 644; "No Place Like Home," *Guardian*, April 29, 2002; "Sharon Aims to Get 1 Million Jews to Move to Israel in Next Few Years," *Ha'aretz*, March 12, 2004.

20. *Dangerous Liaison*, transcript of interview with Aaron and Tamara Deutsch, pp. 10–11.

21. Ibid., p. 39.

22. Daniel Ben Simon, "A Family in Morag Is Sure Sharon Has Been Beaten by the Settlers," *Ha'aretz*, April 30, 2004.

23. Vered Levy-Barzilai, "Ben Artzi's Last Stand," *Ha'aretz*, April 30, 2004.

24. Chris McGreal,"Sharon Sacks Hardliners Who Stand in His Way," *Guardian*, June 5, 2004.

25. David Hartman, *Israelis and the Jewish Tradition: An Ancient People Debating Its Future* (New Haven: Yale University Press, 2000), p. 94.

26. Daniel Ben Simon, "A Battle of 'to be or not to be,' " *Ha'aretz*, April 23, 2004.

27. Doron Rosenblum, "Cashing In on Catastrophe," *Ha'aretz*, February 27, 2004.

28. Hartman, *Israelis and the Jewish Tradition*—the critique of messianism forms the starting point of Hartman's attempt to retrieve another Jewish spirit for modern-day Israel.

29. Arthur Hertzberg, *The Zionist Idea* (1959) (Philadelphia: Jewish Publication Society, 1997), p. 100.

30. Scholem, "Toward an Understanding of the Messianic Idea," p. 9.

31. Cited in Aviezer Ravitsky, *Messianism, Zionism and Jewish Religious Radicalism*, trans. Michael Swirsky and Jonathan Chapman (Chicago: University of Chicago Press, 1993), p. 13.

32. Hannah Arendt, "Jewish History, Revised" (1947), in *The Jew as Pariah: Jewish Identity and Politics in the Modern Age* (New York: Grove Press, 1978), p. 97.

33. Arendt, "The Jewish State: Fifty Years After—Where Have Herzl's Politics Led?" (1946), in *The Jew as Pariah*, p. 167.

34. Cited in Shlomo Avineri, *Moses Hess: Prophet of Communism and Zionism* (New York: New York University Press, 1985), pp. 70–72.

35. Edward Said, "Zionism from the Standpoint of Its Victims," in *The Question of Palestine* (1979) (London: Vintage, 1992), p. 88.

36. J. L. Talmon, *The Nature of Jewish History—Its Universal Significance* (Jerusalem: Hillel Foundation, 1957), p. 11.

37. Daniel Barenboim, "The Jewish People Are on a Path Which Makes One Doubt That There Will Always Be a Jewish State in Israel," Emma Brockes, "Wake Up, Israel," extracts from Daniel Barenboim, *A Life in Music*, *Guardian*, September 6, 2002; Yaakov

Perry, "If We Continue to Live by the Sword, We Will Continue to Wallow in the Mud and Destroy Ourselves," Chris McGreal, "Israel on Road to Ruin, Warn Former Shin Bet Chiefs," *Guardian*, November 15, 2003.

38. Sean O'Hagan, "The Sound and the Fury," *Observer*, June 20, 2002.

39. Bensoussan, *Une histoire*, p. 9.

40. Ibid.

41. Scholem, *Sabbatai Sevi*, p. 689.

42. Theodor Herzl, *Altneuland* (1902), *Old-New Land*, Centenary [birth] Edition, trans. Paula Arnold (Haifa: Haifa Publishing Company, 1960).

43. Ibid., p. 218.

44. Chaim Weizmann, "What Is Zionism?" (lecture to London University Zionist Society, March 21, 1909), in *Letters and Papers*, vol. 1, ser. B, ed. Barnett Litvinoff (New Brunswick, N.J.: Transaction Books, 1983), p. 76.

45. Weizmann, "Zionist Policy" (address, September 21, 1919, London, British Zionist Federation), p. 18.

46. Weizmann to Gregory Lurie January 1, 1903, in *Letters and Papers*, vol. 2, ser. A, ed. Barnett Litvinoff (London: Oxford University Press, 1971), p. 145.

47. Weizmann, "Zionism Needs a Living Content" (Paris, March 28, 1914), in *Letters and Papers*, vol. 1, ser. B, p. 118.

48. Sigmund Freud, *Civilization and Its Discontents* (1930), in *Standard Edition of the Complete Psychological Works*, ed. James Strachey, vol. 21 (London: Hogarth, 1961), p. 144.

49. Ibid.

50. Scholem, "Toward an Understanding of the Messianic Idea," p. 2.

51. Weizmann, "Reminiscences of Fifty Years" (Jubilee Celebration of the First Zionist Congress, Basel, August 31, 1947), in *Letters and Papers*, vol. 2, ser. B, p. 657.

52. Weizmann, "A Vision of the Future" (New York, January 16, 1940), in *Letters and Papers*, vol. 2, ser. B, p. 392. Likewise, the revival of messianic belief in the Lubavitch movement in New York occurred in the immediate aftermath of the war—since the Jewish

people had just survived the worst calamity in their three-thousand-year-long history, it seemed a propitious moment for them to be delivered from the sufferings of exile. Taking the reins of the movement at this moment, Rebbe Schneerson was believed by just about every member to be the Messiah. Jonathan Mahler, "Waiting for the Messiah of Eastern Parkway," *New York Times Magazine*, September 21, 2003. My thanks to Tom Levine for this article.

53. Solomon Grayzel, *A History of the Jews: From the Babylonian Exile to the Present* (Philadelphia: Jewish Publication Society of America, 1947), p. 512.

54. Scholem, *Sabbatai Sevi*, p. 67.

55. Ibid., p. 18.

56. Ibid., p. 9.

57. Scholem, "Toward an Understanding of the Messianic Idea," p. 7 (my emphasis).

58. Scholem, *Sabbatai Sevi*, p. 9.

59. Yitzhak Laor, "Before Rafah," *London Review of Books*, June 3, 2004, p. 18.

60. Uri Avnery, "A Maddened Cow," *Gush-Shalom*, July 6, 2002.

61. David Grossman, "The Pope's Visit to Israel" (March 2000), in *Death as a Way of Life: Dispatches from Jerusalem*, trans. Haim Watzman (London: Bloomsbury, 2003), p. 66.

62. Scholem, *Sabbatai Sevi*, p. 29.

63. Scholem, *Major Trends*, p. 261.

64. Scholem, *Sabbatai Sevi*, p. 34.

65. Hartman, *Israelis and the Jewish Tradition*, p. 32.

66. Scholem, *Sabbatai Sevi*, p. 20.

67. Ibid., pp. 67, 42.

68. Aaron David Gordon, "Our Tasks Ahead" (1920), in Hertzberg, *The Zionist Idea*, pp. 381, 369.

69. Abraham Isaac Kook, "Eretz Yisrael," in *Orot Hakadesh* (Jerusalem: Mosad Harav Kook, 1963), p. 9, cited in Eliezer Schweid, *The Land of Israel: National Home or Land of Destiny*, trans. Deborah Greniman, Herzl Press Publication (New York: Associated University Presses, 1985), p. 177.

70. Scholem, *Sabbatai Sevi*, p. 38.

71. Ibid., p. 65.

72. Kook, "The War" (1910–30), from *Orot* (1942), in Hertzberg, *The Zionist Idea*, p. 423.

73. Kook, "Lights for Rebirth" (1910–30), from *Orot* (1942), in ibid., p. 427.

74. Scholem, *Major Trends*, p. 288.

75. Scholem, *Sabbatai Sevi*, p. 281.

76. Scholem, "Toward an Understanding of the Messianic Idea," pp. 18, 29.

77. Scholem, *Sabbatai Sevi*, pp. 40–41.

78. Scholem, *Major Trends*, p. 311; *Sabbatai Sevi*, p. 729.

79. Scholem, "Toward an Understanding of the Messianic Idea," pp. 11–12.

80. Scholem, *Major Trends*, pp. 315, 311.

81. Scholem, *Sabbatai Sevi*, p. 227.

82. Ibid., pp. 64–65.

83. Bensoussan, *Une histoire*, p. 238.

84. Scholem, *Major Trends*, p. 315.

85. Scholem, *Sabbatai Sevi*, pp. 688–90.

86. Weizmann, *Trial and Error: the Autobiography of Chaim Weizmann* (London: Hamish Hamilton, 1949), p. 21.

87. Ibid., p. 21.

88. Weizmann, "Reminiscences of Fifty Years," p. 658.

89. Amos Elon, *Herzl* (London: Weidenfeld and Nicholson, 1975), p. 9.

90. Ibid., p. 5.

91. Herzl, June 17, 1895, *The Complete Diaries of Theodor Herzl*, ed. Raphael Patai, trans. Harry Zohn, 5 vols. (London: Herzl Press; New York: Thomas Yoseloff, 1960), 1:114; wherever it is available, I give the version of the diaries from this English translation but occasionally modify the translation on the basis of the original German: Herzl, *Tagebücher*, 3 vols. (Berlin: Judischer Verlag, 1922–23).

92. Herzl, June 11, 1900, *Complete Diaries*, 3:960.

93. Herzl, June 16, 1895, *Complete Diaries*, 1:105, cited in Elon, *Herzl*, p. 2.

94. Herzl, "Address to Rothschilds," June 13, 1895, *Complete Diaries*, 1:130, cited in Elon, *Herzl*, p. 147.

95. Reuben Brainin, *Chajen Herzl* (*Herzl's Life*) (New York, 1919), 1:18, cited in Elon, *Herzl*, p. 16.

96. Scholem, *Sabbatai Sevi*, p. 164.

97. Herzl, June 7 and 8, 1895, *Complete Diaries*, 1:38, 41, cited in Elon, *Herzl*, p. 145. Herzl also proclaimed to Moritz Güdemann, "I will make you the first bishop of the capital," June 7, 1895, *Complete Diaries*, 1:37.

98. Cited in Elon, *Herzl*, p. 145.

99. Herzl to Julie Naschauser, June 11, 1895, cited in Elon, *Herzl*, p. 145.

100. Weizmann, *Trial and Error*, p. 61.

101. Herzl, August 18, 1895, *Complete Diaries*, 1:232, cited in Elon, *Herzl*, p. 227.

102. Ben-Gurion, *Igrot* (*Letters*), 1:20, cited in Elon, *Herzl*, p. 402.

103. Cited in David Vital, *The Origins of Zionism* (Oxford: Oxford University Press, 1975), p. 244.

104. Yerahmiel Domb, *Ha-Homah* (*The Wall*) (1975), pp. 94–95, cited in Ravitsky, *Messianism, Zionism*, p. 73 (emphasis original).

105. Bensoussan, *Une histoire*, p. 93.

106. Ravitsky, *Messianism, Zionism*, p. 35.

107. Max Nordau, "Zionism" (1902), in Hertzberg, *The Zionist Idea*, p. 242.

108. Ibid.

109. Herzl, *Zionist Writings*, trans. Harry Zohn, 2 vols. (London: Herzl Press, 1973–75), 1:132, cited in Michael Berkowitz, *Zionist Culture and West European Jewry before the First World War* (Cambridge: Cambridge University Press, 1993).

110. Yehudah Burla, exchange with Scholem in *Davar*, November–December 1929, cited in David Biale, *Gershom Scholem: Kabbalah and Counter-History* (Cambridge: Harvard University Press, 1979), p. 177.

111. Ravitsky, *Messianism, Zionism*; Ehud Sprinzak, "Three Models of Religious Violence: The Case of Jewish Fundamentalism in Israel," in *Fundamentalisms and the State: Remaking Polities, Economies and Militance*, ed. Martin Murray and R. Scott Appleby (Chicago: University of Chicago Press, 1993); Schweid, *The Land of Israel*; Ian S. Lustick, "Jewish Fundamentalism and the Israeli-Pales-

tinian Impasse," in *Jewish Fundamentalism in Comparative Perspective: Religion, Ideology and the Crisis of Modernity*, ed. Laurence J. Silberstein (New York: New York University Press, 1993).

112. Bensoussan, *Une histoire*, p. 498.

113. Biale, *Gershom Sholem*, p. 184.

114. Hartman, *Israelis and the Jewish Tradition*, p. 6.

115. Ravitsky, *Messianism, Zionism*, pp. 5–6.

116. Ibid., pp. 37–38.

117. Rabbi Shlomo Aviner, "Messianic Realism," in *Whole Homeland: Eretz Israel Roots of the Jewish Claim* (Jerusalem: Department for Torah Education and Culture in the Diaspora, World Zionist Organization, 1978), pp. 115–16, cited in Lustick, "Jewish Fundamentalism," p. 112.

118. Sprinzak, "Three Models of Religious Violence," p. 474.

119. I am indebted here to Ravitsky's discussion of the Harbingers, *Messianism, Zionism*, pp. 27–32.

120. Yehuda Alkalai, "The Third Redemption" (1843), in Hertzberg, *The Zionist Idea*, p. 105.

121. Ibid.

122. Hartman, *Israelis and the Jewish Tradition*, p. 149.

123. Gordon, cited in Schweid, *The Land of Israel*, p. 163.

124. Nadav Shragai, "This Land Is Our Land," *Ha'aretz*, June 25, 2004, p. 10.

125. Gordon, cited in Schweid, *The Land of Israel*, p. 167.

126. Ibid., p. 186.

127. Weizmann, "The Jewish People and Palestine," p. 27.

128. Scholem, *Sabbatai Sevi*, p. 46 (my emphasis).

129. Kalischer, cited in Ravitsky, *Messianism, Zionism*, p. 30.

130. David Ben-Gurion, *Israel: A Personal History*, trans. Nechemia Meyers and Uzy Nystar (London: New English Library, 1972), p. 818.

131. Weizmann, "Reminiscences," Czernowitz, December 12, 1927, in Hertzberg, *The Zionist Idea*, p. 580.

132. Weizmann, *Trial and Error*, p. 63.

133. Ibid.

134. Ibid., p. 418.

135. Weizmann, "The Cultural Question in Zionism" (speech to Fourth Zionist Congress, August 16, 1900), in *Letters and Papers*, vol. 1, ser. B, p. 3.

136. Weizmann, "Reminiscences," in Hertzberg, *The Zionist Idea*, p. 578.

137. Scholem, *Sabbatai Sevi*, p. 284.

138. Maurice Edelman, *Ben-Gurion: A Political Biography* (London: Hodder and Stoughton, 1964), p. 33.

139. Scholem to Franz Rosenzweig, 1926, cited in Ravitsky, *Messianism, Zionism*, p. 35.

140. Declaration of Independence of the State of Israel, cited in Ben-Gurion, *Israel*, p. 81.

141. Rabbi Zvi Tau, cited in Ravitsky, *Messianism, Zionism*, p. 83.

142. Rashi, BT Sanhedrin 98a, cited in ibid., p. 38.

143. Cited in Bensoussan, *Une histoire*, p. 138.

144. Ben-Gurion, *Israel*, p. 24.

145. Scholem, "Toward an Understanding of the Messianic Idea," p. 35.

146. Avnery, "Children of Death" (June 14, 2003); "The Murder of Arafat" (March 30, 2002), *Gush-Shalom*.

147. Ben-Gurion, *Israel*, pp. 25–26.

148. Ibid., p. xix.

149. Kook, "Eretz Yisrael," cited in Schweid, *The Land of Israel*, p. 177.

150. Hertzberg, *The Zionist Idea*, pp. 74–75.

151. Ben-Gurion, "The Forefathers of the Jewish Nation" (typescript, Jerusalem, 1950), p. 1.

152. Ben-Gurion, "Socialist Zionism," in *Selections* (New York: Labor Zionist Organization of America, Paole Zion, 1948), p. 27 (my emphasis).

153. Ibid.

154. Ben-Gurion, Statement before the Royal Commission (Jerusalem, 1936); *Israel*, p. 803.

155. See Mitchell Cohen, *Zion and State: Nation, Class and the Shaping of Modern Israel* (Oxford: Blackwell, 1987), esp. pt. 3, "Statehood,"chap. 11, "Mamlakhtiyut I: Of Golden Calves and Mes-

siahs," chap. 12, "Mamlakhtiyut II: From *Am Oved* to *Am Mamlakhti*"; I am grateful to Olga Litwak for telling me about this book.

156. Avineri, "Israel in the Post-Ben-Gurion Ethic: The Nemesis of Messianism," *Midstream*, September 1965, p. 23, cited in ibid., p. 207.

157. Ben-Gurion, "The State and the Future of Zionism" (address to the Zionist General Council, Jerusalem, 1950), cited in ibid., p. 209.

158. Hertzberg, *The Zionist Idea*, p. 79.

159. Ben-Gurion, "Science and Ethics: The Contributions of Greece, India and Israel," in *Convocation Honoring Ben-Gurion* (Waltham, Mass.: Brandeis University Publications, 1960), p. 11.

160. Scholem, "Toward an Understanding of the Messianic Idea," p. 15.

161. Nathan Shapira, *The Goodness of the Land* (1655), cited in Scholem, *Sabbatai Sevi*, p. 74.

162. Ibid.

163. Ibid., p. 14.

164. Ben-Gurion, "The New Tasks of World Zionism" (opening session of Zionist General Council [Actions Committee], Jerusalem, 1949) (London: Zionist Information Office, 1949), p. 1; "Principles for the Jewish State" (address to the Executive of Mapai, December 3, 1947), in *Selections*, p. 75. Even if he allows in his speech to the Zionist General Council that the Israeli government is not qualified to speak on behalf of world Jewry, yet it is the task of Zionists in free countries to show that their Zionism is no "lip-service" but a "revolutionary impulse aimed at the ingathering of the exiles" (p. 7). On the twentieth anniversary of the founding of Israel, Ben-Gurion cites the speech he had given to a convened group of intellectuals, teachers, and scientists one week after the end of the 1948 war: "The State of Israel has another element that is unique—the redemption of the people of Israel and the ingathering of the exiles' (*Israel*, p. 822). "I am now engaged in writing a history of Israel since the year 1870, when French Jews established an agricultural school named Mikve Israel (which in Hebrew means both 'the hope of Israel' and 'Israel's ingathering')." *Israel*, p. 804.

165. Ben-Gurion, *Israel*, p. 41.

166. Ben-Gurion, address to the Central Committee of the Histadrut (December 30 1947), cited in Nur Masalha, *Expulsion of the Palestinians: The Concept of "Transfer" in Zionist Political Thought, 1882–1948* (Washington, D.C.: Institute for Palestine Studies, 1992), p. 176.

167. Weizmann to Jewish Telegraphic Agency, quoted in Oskar K. Rabinowicz, *Fifty Years of Zionism: A Historical Analysis of Dr. Weizmann's Trial and Error* (London: Robert Anscombe, 1950), p. 80.

168. Cited in Said, "Zionism from the Standpoint of Its Victims," p. 100.

169. Aviner, "Messianic Realism," cited in Lustick, "Jewish Fundamentalism," p. 112.

170. Shragai, "This Land Is Our Land," p. 11.

171. Ben-Gurion, *Israel*, p. 46 (emphasis original).

172. Ibid., p. 816 (my emphasis).

173. Ibid., p. 839.

174. Orit Shohat, "A Democratic, Not Demographic, Threat," *Ha'aretz*, July 23, 2004.

175. Neri Livneh, "How 90 Peruvians Became the Latest Jewish Settlers," *Guardian*, August 7, 2002.

176. Jonathan Lis, "Private Plan Would See New Jewish Neighbourhood South of Jerusalem," *Ha'aretz*, June 11, 2004.

177. W. R. Bion, "Group Dynamics: A Re-view," in *New Directions in Psycho-Analysis: The Significance of Infant Conflict in the Pattern of Adult Behaviour*, ed. Melanie Klein, Paula Heimann, and R. E. Money-Kyrle (1955) (London: Maresfield, 1977).

178. Ibid., p. 449.

179. Ibid., p. 457.

180. Israel Shahak and Norton Mezvinsky, *Jewish Fundamentalism in Israel* (London: Pluto, 1999); Israel Shahak, *Jewish History, Jewish Religion* (London: Pluto, 1994).

181. Schweid, *The Land of Israel*, p. 198.

182. Scholem, *Judaica*, 3 vols. (Frankfurt, 1968–73), 1:146, cited in Biale, *Gershom Scholem*, pp. 173–74.

183. Scholem to Benjamin, August 1, 1931, in Scholem, *Walter Benjamin: The Story of a Friendship*, trans. Harry Zohn (New York: Schocken, 1981), p. 172.

184. Scholem, "Three Sins of Brit Shalom," *Davar*, November 24, 1929, p. 2, cited in Biale, *Gershom Scholem*, p. 177; Scholem cited in ibid., p. 181.

185. Scholem, *The Fullness of Time*, trans. Richard Sieburth (Jerusalem: Ibis, 2003), pp. 87–89.

186. Benjamin Netanyahu, *A Place among the Nations: Israel and the World* (New York: Bantam, 1993), p. 364.

187. Abraham Stern, poet and leader of Lehi (Freedom Fighters of Israel), the radical Revisionist group that broke with the Irgun in 1940, described himself as a soldier of the King Messiah, charged with forcing the end.

188. Netanyahu, *A Place among the Nations*, p. 364.

189. Ibid.

190. Scholem, "Toward an Understanding of the Messianic Idea," p. 36.

191. Scholem to Benjamin, in *Walter Benjamin*, p. 173.

Chapter 2
"Imponderables in thin air": Zionism as Psychoanalysis (Critique)

1. Herzl, *Altneuland.*
2. Ibid., p. 19.
3. Ibid., p. 24.
4. Ibid.
5. Ibid., p. 29.
6. Ibid., p. 34.
7. Ibid., p. 53.
8. Ibid., p. 70.
9. Ibid., p. 104.
10. Ibid., p. 54.
11. Ibid., p. 100.
12. *Dangerous Liaison*, transcript of interview with Yossi Beilin, p. 21.

13. Herzl, October 9, 1898, *Complete Diaries*, 2:702.

14. Herzl, June 12, 1895, ibid., 1:88, *Tagebücher*, 1:98: "Die arme Bevölkerung trachten wir unbemerkt über die Grenze zu schaffen," cited in Masalha, *Expulsion of the Palestinians*, p. 9.

15. Jonathan Sacks, *The Dignity of Difference: How to Avoid the Clash of Civilisations* (London: Continuum, 2002).

16. Herzl, *Altneuland*, p. 100.

17. Ibid., p. 62.

18. Elon, *Herzl*, p. 7.

19. Herzl, *Diaries*, September 4, 1879, cited in Elon, *Herzl*, pp. 44–45.

20. Scholem, *Sabbatai Sevi*, p. 127.

21. Herzl, June 16 and 2, 1895, Pentecost, *Complete Diaries*, 1:104, 3, cited in Elon, *Herzl*, p. 3.

22. Elon, *Herzl*, p. 2.

23. Herzl, April 16, 1896, June 5, 1895, *Complete Diaries*, 1:24, 33, cited in Elon, *Herzl*, p. 2.

24. Herzl, June 11, 1895, *Complete Diaries*, 1:75, cited in Elon, *Herzl*, p. 2.

25. Weizmann, letter to Leo Motzkin, January 31, 1902, in *Letters and Papers*, vol. 1, ser. A, ed. Leonard Stein, in collaboration with Gedalia Yogev (London: Oxford University Press, 1968), p. 224.

26. Weizmann, letter to Vera Khatzman, July 6–7, 1901, in ibid., p. 153.

27. Israel has never wished the children of Herzl to be buried on Mount Herzl, even when offers to do so were made.

28. Hess, *Rome and Jerusalem* (1862), in Hertzberg, *The Zionist Idea*, p. 119.

29. Bensoussan, *Une histoire*, p. 407.

30. Max Nordau to Herzl, February 26, 1896, cited in Vital, *The Origins of Zionism*, p. 269.

31. Arendt, "The Jewish State: Fifty Years After," p. 165.

32. Leon Pinsker, *AutoEmancipation! An Appeal to His People by a Russian Jew* (1882), in Hertzberg, *The Zionist Idea*, p. 192.

33. A. D. Gordon, "Final Reflections" (1921), in ibid., p. 384.

34. Sigmund Freud, *The Interpretation of Dreams* (1900), Standard Edition, 4:48.

35. Arendt, "Zionism Reconsidered" (1944), in *The Jew as Pariah*, p. 138.

36. Cited in Bensoussan, *Une histoire*, p. 474.

37. Ibid.

38. Herzl, conversation with Maurice de Hirsch, June 2, 1895, Pentecost, *Complete Diaries*, 1:19, *Tagebücher*, 1:22, cited in Elon, *Herzl*, p. 136.

39. Herzl to de Hirsch, June 3, 1895, *Complete Diaries*, 1:27–28, *Tagebücher*, 1:33, cited in Elon, *Herzl*, p. 137 (my emphasis).

40. Herzl to de Hirsch, June 3, 1895, *Complete Diaries*, 1:27, *Tagebücher*, 1:32, cited in Elon, *Herzl*, p. 143.

41. Amnon Raz-Krakotzkin, "Binationalism and Jewish Identity: Hannah Arendt and the Question of Palestine," in *Hannah Arendt in Jerusalem*, ed. Stephen E. Aschheim (Berkeley and Los Angeles: University of California Press, 2001), p. 169.

42. Martin Buber, "Zionism and 'Zionism' " (1948), in *A Land of Two Peoples: Martin Buber on Jews and Arabs*, ed. Paul Mendes-Flohr (New York: Oxford University Press, 1983), p. 220.

43. Ibid., p. 221.

44. Ibid.

45. Arendt, "Zionism Reconsidered," p. 146.

46. Martin Buber, "The Spirit of Israel and the World of Today" (1939), in *On Judaism*, ed. Nahum N. Glatzer (New York: Schocken, 1967), p. 185.

47. Buber, "Zionism and 'Zionism,' " p. 221.

48. Ibid.

49. Ibid., p. 223.

50. Ibid., p. 221.

51. Said, "Zionism from the Standpoint of Its Victims," p. 89 (emphasis original).

52. "What Needs to Be Done," announcement of opening Conference of the Sikkuy "Or Commission Watch" Project, *Ha'aretz*, June 18, 2004.

53. Buber, "Should the Ichud Accept the Decree of History?" (1949), in Mendes-Flohr, *A Land of Two Peoples*, p. 250.

54. David Grossman, "Death as a Way of Life" (May 2001), in *Death as a Way of Life*, p. 115.

55. Buber, "Politics and Morality" (1945), in Mendes-Flohr, *A Land of Two Peoples*, p. 172.

56. Freud, "The Dissection of the Psychical Personality," Lecture 31, in *New Introductory Lectures* (1933), Standard Edition, 22:80.

57. Jacques Lacan, "The Freudian Thing" (1955), in *Ecrits: A Selection*, trans. Alan Sheridan (London: Tavistock, 1977), pp. 128–29.

58. Buber, "The Spirit of Israel and the World of Today," p. 180 (my emphasis).

59. Hans Kohn, "Nationalism" (1921–22), in *The Jew: Essays from Buber's Journal Der Jude*, ed. Arthur A. Cohen, trans. Joachim Neugroschel (Tuscaloosa: University of Alabama Press, 1980), p. 27 (my emphasis).

60. For a discussion of the emergence of messianism in German-Jewish thought after the First World War, see Anson Rabinbach, *In the Shadow of Catastrophe: German Intellectuals between Apocalypse and Enlightenment* (Berkeley and Los Angeles: University of California Press, 1977). Rabinbach shows how the radical messianism of Walter Benjamin and Ernest Bloch, apocalyptic and esoteric, with its "certitude of redemption" and "bleak pessimism" after the First World War, progressively detached itself from political and hence any nationalist aspirations (p. 62). See esp. chap. 1 "Between Apocalypse and Enlightenment: Benjamin, Bloch and Modern German-Jewish Messianism."

61. Arnold Zweig, *The Face of East European Jewry*, ed. and trans. Noah Isenberg (Berkeley and Los Angeles: University of California Press, 2004), p. 11.

62. Buber, "The Meaning of Zionism" (1946), in Mendes-Flohr, *A Land of Two Peoples*, p. 183.

63. Ibid.

64. Buber, "Zionism and 'Zionism,' " p. 222.

65. Ibid.

66. Ibid., p. 221.

67. Herzl to de Hirsch, June 3, 1895, *Complete Diaries*, 1:27, cited in Elon, *Herzl*, p. 137.

68. Weizmann, *Trial and Error*, p. 418; "On World Citizenship and Nationalism" (Prague, March 27, 1912), in *Letters and Papers*,

vol. 1, ser. B, pp. 89, 91; "The Jewish People and Palestine," p. 12; "States Are Not Given" (address at UPA Campaign Banquet, London, January 28, 1948), in *Letters and Papers*, vol. 1, ser. B,, p. 687. (My emphasis throughout.)

69. Hans Kohn, "Zionism Is Not Judaism" (1929), in Mendes-Flohr, *A Land of Two Peoples*, p. 98.

70. Ibid.

71. Ibid., p. 99.

72. Buber, "Our Reply" (response to an attack by the clandestine military group, the Irgun, in their underground publication, *Herut* [Freedom] on Buber's organization, the Ichud, 1945), in Mendes-Flohr, *A Land of Two Peoples*; "Should the Ichud Accept the Decree of History?" pp. 178, 248.

73. Kohn, "Zionism Is Not Judaism," p. 99.

74. Ibid.

75. Kohn, "Zionism," in *Living in a World Revolution: My Encounters with History* (New York: Trident, 1964), p. 48; my thanks to Elliott Ratzman for giving me this volume.

76. Kohn, "Nationalism," pp. 30, 96.

77. Ibid., editor's note, p. 20.

78. Ibid., p. 26.

79. Hermione Lee, *Virginia Woolf* (London: Chatto, 1996), p. 510.

80. Kohn, "Nationalism," p. 26.

81. Ibid., p. 28.

82. Ibid.

83. Ibid., p. 26.

84. Ibid., p. 25; Freud, *The Future of an Illusion* (1927), Standard Edition, 21:18.

85. Judah Leon Magnes, "Like All the Nations?" (1930), in Mendes-Flohr, *A Land of Two Peoples*, p. 447.

86. Freud, *The Future of an Illusion*, p. 34; Kohn, "Nationalism," p. 27.

87. Edward Said, *Freud and the Non-European* (London: Verso and the Freud Museum, 2003).

88. Kohn, "Nationalism," p. 27.

89. Leon Pinsker, *AutoEmancipation!*, in Hertzberg, *The Zionist Idea*, pp. 184, 194.

90. Buber, "Should the Ichud Accept the Decree of History?" p. 250 (my emphasis).

91. Arendt, "Zionism Reconsidered," p. 156.

92. Ibid., p. 172.

93. Ibid., p. 156.

94. Ibid., pp. 132–33.

95. Ibid., p. 133.

96. Ibid., p. 162.

97. *Dangerous Liaison*, transcript of interview with Ramadan Safi, p. 5. See also Noam Chomsky, *Fateful Triangle: The United States, Israel and the Palestinians* (1993; rev. ed., London: Pluto, 1999).

98. Talmon, *Israel among the Nations*, pp. 102–3.

99. Arendt, "Zionism Reconsidered," p. 141.

100. Tom Nairn, "Out of the Cage," *London Review of Books*, June 24, 2004, p. 14.

101. Kohn, "Nationalism," p. 30.

102. Arendt, "To Save the Jewish Homeland—There Is Still Time" (May 1948), in *The Jew as Pariah*, p. 187.

103. Ronit Chacham, *Breaking Ranks: Refusing to Serve in the West Bank and Gaza Strip* (New York: Other Press, 2003), p. 60.

104. McGreal, "Israel on Road to Ruin."

105. Gideon Levy, "I Punched an Arab in the Face," *Ha'aretz*, November 21, 2003, p. 7.

106. Ze'ev Schiff, "Crazy after All These Years," *Ha'aretz*, March 26, 2003.

107. Cited in Colin Urquhart, "Hamas Barrage Follows Israeli Raid," *Guardian*, October 22, 2003.

108. Ari Shavit, "On the Eve of Destruction" (interview with Avraham Burg), *Ha'aretz*, November 14, 2003, p. 4.

109. Kohn, "Nationalism," p. 20.

110. Jonathan Spyer, "Israel's Demographic Timebomb," *Guardian*, January 14, 2004.

111. Ilan Pappe, "Encountering Nationalism: The Urge for Cohabitation," in *A History of Modern Palestine: One Land, Two Peoples* (Cambridge: Cambridge University Press, 2004), p. 116. See

also Susan Lee Hattis, *The Bi-National Idea in Palestine during Mandatory Times* (Tel Aviv: Shikmona Press, 1970).

112. Samuels to Smuts, March 30, 1948, cited in Hattis, *The Bi-National Idea*, p. 316.

113. Peter Hirschberg, "One-State Awakening," *Ha'aretz*, December 12, 2003, p. 14.

114. Cited in N. de M. Bentwich, *Ahad Ha'am and His Philosophy* (Jerusalem: Keren Hayesod [Palestine Foundation Fund] and the Keren Kayemeth Le-Israel, 1927), p. 22.

115. Cited in ibid. (my emphasis).

116. Kohn, "Zionism Is Not Judaism," p. 99.

117. Ahad Ha'am to Weizmann, quoted in Yosef Gorny, *Israel and the Arabs 1882–1948: A Study of Ideology* (Oxford: Clarendon, 1987), p. 63.

118. Ahad Ha'am, "The Truth from Palestine" (1891), cited in Steven J. Zipperstein, *Elusive Prophet: Ahad Ha'am and the Origins of Zionism*, Jewish Thinkers, gen. ed. Arthur Hertzberg (London: Peter Halban, 1993), p. 57.

119. Bentwich, *Ahad Ha'am*, p. 5; Zipperstein, *Elusive Prophet*, p. xxiii, Hertzberg, *The Zionist Idea*, p. 250.

120. Cited in Zipperstein, *Elusive Prophet*, p. 196.

121. Ahad Ha'am, "The Truth from Palestine," cited in ibid., p. 61.

122. Ahad Ha'am to Moshe Smilansky, November 18, 1913, cited in Kohn, "Zionism," p. 54.

123. Ahad Ha'am, "The Wrong Way" (1889), *Nationalism and the Jewish Ethic: Basic Writings of Ahad Ha'am*, ed. and introd. Hans Kohn (New York: Schocken, 1962), p. 35.

124. Ahad Ha'am, "Positive and Negative," in *Selected Essays*, trans. Leon Simon (Philadelphia: Jewish Publication Society of America, 1912), p. 52.

125. Scholem to Benjamin, August 1, 1931, in *Walter Benjamin*, p. 173.

126. Ahad Ha'am, "Moses" (1904), in *Essays, Letters, Memoirs*, trans. and ed. Leon Simon, East West Library (Oxford: Oxford University Press, 1946), p. 327.

127. For a discussion of Franz Rosenzweig's critique of this issue, and the question of idolatry in relation to political fulfillment, see Leora Batnitzky, *Idolatry and Representation: The Philosophy of Franz Rosenzweig Reconsidered* (Princeton: Princeton University Press, 2000).

128. Ahad Ha'am, "Moses," p. 323.

129. Ibid., p. 324.

130. Magnes, "Like All the Nations?" p. 447; Arendt, "Zionism Reconsidered," pp. 171, 166.

131. Herzl to Güdemann, June 16, 1895, *Complete Diaries*, 1:112.

132. Herzl, *The Jewish State: An Attempt at a Modern Solution of the Jewish Question* (1896), trans. Sylvie D'Avigdor, 2nd ed. (London: Central Office of the Zionist Organisation, 1934), p. 20.

133. Herzl, conversation with de Hirsch, June 2, 1895, *Complete Diaries*, 1:21.

134. Ahad Ha'am, "The Wrong Way," p. 40.

135. Ahad Ha'am, "A Spiritual Centre" (1907), in *Essays, Letters, Memoirs*, p. 205.

136. Ahad Ha'am, "Two Masters," in *Selected Essays*, p. 100.

137. Ahad Ha'am, "A Spiritual Centre," p. 206.

138. Ahad Ha'am, "Past and Future" (1891), in *Selected Essays*, p. 87.

139. Ibid., p. 81.

140. Frédéric Paulhan, *L'activité mentale et les éléments de l'esprit* (Paris: Felix Alcan, 1889), pt. 3, *L'esprit*, bk. 1, *Synthèse concrète*, chap. 2, "Synthèses générale—la formation de la personnalité—Darwin," p. 484.

141. Ibid., introduction, p. 7.

142. Ibid., pt. 3, bk. 1, chap. 1, "Synthèses partielles—l'amour, la langue," pp. 282–83.

143. Ibid., pt. 3, bk. 1, chap. 2, p. 504.

144. Paulhan, *Les mensonges du caractère* (Paris: Felix Alcan, 1905), p. 107.

145. Ibid., p. 109.

146. Ahad Ha'am, "Two Masters," p. 91.

147. Ibid.

148. Ibid., p. 92.

149. Ibid.

150. Ibid., p. 102.

151. Ibid.

152. Ibid., p. 94.

153. Siegfried Lehmann, "Zionism and Irrationality," in *Shorashim* (*Roots*) (1943), cited in Bensoussan, *Une histoire*, p. 777.

154. Ahad Ha'am, "Two Masters," p. 99.

155. Robert Louis Stevenson, *The Strange Case of Dr Jekyll and Mr Hyde* (1881) (Oxford: Oxford University Press, 1987), p. 61.

156. Lacan, "Intervention on Transference" (1951), in *Feminine Sexuality: Jacques Lacan and the Ecole Freudienne*, ed. Juliet Mitchell and Jacqueline Rose, trans. Jacqueline Rose (London: Macmillan, 1982), p. 72.

157. Chisin, February 10, 1882, *A Palestine Diary: Memoirs of a Bilau Pioneer 1881–1887* (New York, 1976), cited in Josef Frankel, *Prophecy and Politics: Socialism, Nationalism and the Russian Jews 1862–1917* (Cambridge: Cambridge University Press, 1981), p. 92.

158. *Dangerous Liaison*, typescript of interview with Aaron and Tamara Deutsch, p. 6.

159. Yosef Hayim Yerushalmi, *Zakhor: Jewish History and Jewish Memory* (1982) (Seattle: University of Washington Press, 1996), p. 8.

160. *Dangerous Liaison*, interview with Aaron and Tamara Deutsch, p. 12.

161. Shragai, "This Land Is Our Land," p. 10.

162. Compare the moment in the 1950s, recalled by psychoanalyst Christopher Bollas at the opening of his book *The Shadow of the Object* (New York: Columbia University Press, 1987), when Paula Heimann, a member of the British Psycho-Analytic Society, posed a simple question about the patient in analysis: "Who is speaking?" "Up until this moment it had always been assumed that the speaker was the patient," Bollas comments. "But Heimann knew that at any given moment in a session a patient could be speaking with the voice of the mother, or the mood of the father, or some fragmented voice

of a child self either lived or withheld from life" (p. 1). My thanks to Martin Golding for pointing out this similarity.

163. Ahad Ha'am, "Imitation and Assimilation" (1893), in *Selected Essays*, pp. 107–8.

164. Ibid., pp. 113–14.

165. Ahad Ha'am, "A Spiritual Centre," p. 203.

166. Ahad Ha'am, "Imitation and Assimilation," p. 112.

167. Ibid.

168. Ahad Ha'am, "Moses," p. 315.

169. Kohn, "Nationalism," p. 27.

170. Weizmann, "A Vision of the Future," p. 389.

171. Ahad Ha'am, "Ancestor Worship," in *Selected Essays*, p. 208.

172. Ibid., p. 209.

173. Ibid.

174. Freud, *The Interpretation of Dreams*, p. 68; translation taken here from the Oxford University Press edition (1999), trans. Joyce Crick, p. 58.

175. Ahad Ha'am, "Ancestor Worship," p. 209.

176. Ibid.

177. Levy, "I Punched an Arab in the Face," p. 6.

178. McGreal, "Israel on Road to Ruin"; Amir Oren, "The Fire Next Time," *Ha'aretz*, March 26, 2004.

179. In addition to Ronit Chacham, *Breaking Ranks*, see also *Refusenik! Israel's Soldiers of Conscience*, ed. Peretz Kidron (New York: Zed, 2004).

180. Aviv Lavie, "Hebron Diaries," *Ha'aretz*, June 18, 2004, p. 10; see also, for extracts from the catalog, Yitzhak Laor, "In Hebron," *London Review of Books*, July 22, 2004.

181. Moshe Nissim, "I Made Them a Stadium in the Middle of the Camp," *Yediot Aharanot*, May 31, 2002, *Gush-Shalom*, June 17, 2002, p. 5.

182. Chacham, *Breaking Ranks*, p. 60.

183. Gordon, "Some Observations" (1911), in Hertzberg, *The Zionist Idea*, p. 377.

184. Buber, "Politics and Morality," p. 171.

185. Ibid.
186. Ibid., editor's note, p. 175.
187. Arendt, "The Jewish State: Fifty Years After," p. 175.
188. Ibid.
189. *Dangerous Liaison*, typescript of interview with Naomi Chazan, p. 28.
190. Buber, "And If Not Now, When?" (1932), in Mendes-Flohr, *A Land of Two Peoples*, p. 104.
191. Rabbis for Human Rights, "Dear Prime Minister Sharon," *Ha'aretz*, March 19, 2004.
192. Marc H. Ellis, *Israel and Palestine Out of the Ashes: The Search for Jewish Identity in the Twenty-First Century* (London: Pluto, 2002), pp. 35, 138.

Chapter 3
"Break their bones": Zionism as Politics (Violence)

1. I use Elon's translation, which is much closer to the spirit of the German than the English version: "Ich hetzte die Leute allmählich in die Staatstimmung."
2. Herzl, June 12, 1895, *Complete Diaries*, 1:83.
3. Steven Beller, *Vienna and the Jews, 1867–1938: A Cultural History* (Cambridge: Cambridge University Press, 1989), p. 195.
4. Report in the *Neue Freie Presse*, February 6, 1895, cited in Elon, *Herzl*, p. 129.
5. Herzl, draft of speech to Rothschilds, June 13, 1895, *Complete Diaries*, 1:171, cited in Elon, *Herzl*, p. 148.
6. Ibid.
7. Herzl, October 8, 1898, *Complete Diaries*, 2:694–95, *Tagebücher*, 2:152, cited in Elon, *Herzl*, p. 277.
8. Herzl to Julie Naschauser, cited in Elon, *Herzl*, p. 115.
9. Herzl, Pentecost, June 2, 1895, *Complete Diaries*, 1:7, cited in Elon, *Herzl*, p. 115.
10. Herzl, Pentecost, June 2, 1895, *Complete Diaries*, 1:10.
11. Herzl, *The Jewish State*, p. 20.
12. Herzl to Güdemann, June 16, 1895, *Complete Diaries*, 1:110, also in letter to Bismark, "I believe I have found the solution to the

Jewish question. Not *a* solution, but *the* solution, the only one." June 19, 1895, *Complete Diaries*, 1:118.

13. Herzl, meeting with the kaiser, cited in Elon, *Herzl*, p. 193.

14. Herzl, April 23 and 25, 1896, *Complete Diaries*, 1:334–35, 337.

15. Herzl, June 12, 1895, ibid., p. 83.

16. Kaiser Wilhelm II, *Memoir*, cited in Elon, *Herzl*, p. 301.

17. P. M. Nevlinski reporting the sultan, April 23, 1896, *Complete Diaries*, 1:118, cited in Elon, *Herzl*, p. 200.

18. Herzl, *The Jewish State*, p. 24; "Address to Rothschilds," June 15, 1895, *Complete Diaries*, 1:180.

19. Ahad Ha'am, "Two Masters," p. 104.

20. Ahad Ha'am, "Progress and Anti-Semitism" (1898), in *Essays, Letters, Memoirs*, p. 210.

21. Weizmann, *Trial and Error*, p. 47.

22. Herzl, Pentecost, 1895, *Complete Diaries*, 1:9, cited in Elon, *Herzl*, p. 121.

23. Ahad Ha'am, "Progress and Anti-Semitism," p. 209.

24. Kohn, "Nationalism," p. 26.

25. In a letter to Moritz Güdemann of 1895, Herzl traces the beginning of his preoccupation to 1882: "How did I discover [the Jewish question]? I do not know. Probably because I pondered it all the time and felt so unhappy about anti-Semitism." Letter to Güdemann, June 16, 1895, *Complete Diaries*, 1:111. In the entry of June 2, 1895, he describes two episodes, one in Mainz in 1888 and one in Baden near Vienna when someone shouted out "Dirty Jew" as he rode home in a carriage, as being decisive, *Complete Diaries*, 1:6.

26. Herzl, *The Jewish State*, p. 26 (my emphasis).

27. Heinrich Graetz, *History of the Jews* vol. 11 (1856–76), cited in Elon, *Herzl*, p. 40 (my emphasis).

28. Minutes of the Zionist Organization, May 8, 1922 (Zionist Central Archives, Jerusalem), cited in Bensoussan, *Une histoire*, p. 781. "Yishuv" refers to the Jewish settlement in Palestine before the founding of the state.

29. Ben-Gurion, "Imperatives of the Jewish Revolution" (1944), in Hertzberg, *The Zionist Idea*, p. 690.

30. Ben-Gurion, *Israel*, p. 80.

31. Edward Said, "Bases for Coexistence" (1997), in *The End of the Peace Process: Oslo and After* (London: Granta, 2000).

32. Chris McGreal, " 'I can't imagine anyone who considers himself a human being can do this,' " *Guardian*, July 28, 2003.

33. Herzl, *Altneuland*, p. 29.

34. David Grossman, "Suddenly Human Contact" (1993), in *Death as a Way of Life*, p. 2.

35. Yossi Safed, "The Night of the Broken Clubs," *Ha'aretz*, May 4, 1989, cited in Ellis, *Israel and Palestine Out of the Ashes*, p. 39.

36. Ben-Gurion, "Imperatives of the Jewish Revolution," p. 609 (my emphasis).

37. Ben-Gurion, *Israel*, p. xx.

38. Ibid., p. 6.

39. Job 40:4, 42:6.

40. Ben-Gurion, *Israel*, p. 72 (my emphasis).

41. For a full discussion of this moment, see Pappe, *The Making of the Arab-Israeli Conflict 1947–1951* (New York: St. Martin's, 1992), chap. 1, "The Diplomatic Battle."

42. Alan Reich, "Cries of Pain from Jenin," *Jewish Quarterly* 195 (Autumn 2004).

43. Weizmann, "Zionist Policy," pp. 22, 7, 10.

44. Weizmann, "The Jewish People and Palestine," p. 27.

45. Job 38:26–28, 40:9.

46. Alkalai, "The Third Redemption," p. 105.

47. Weizmann, "Zionist Policy," p. 13.

48. Ben-Gurion, *Israel*, p. 43.

49. Weizmann, "Awaiting the Shaw Report" (1930), Paper 116, in *Letters and Papers*, vol. 1, ser. B, p. 591; Weizmann to Jan Smuts, February 26, 1943, in Richard Stevens, *Weizmann and Smuts: A Study in Zionist-South African Cooperation* (Washington, D.C.: Institute for Palestine Studies, 1975), app. 1, p. 117; "Awaiting the Shaw Report," p. 598.

50. Weizmann, "A Vision of the Future," p. 389.

51. Weizmann, "Zionist Policy," p. 11.

52. Bensoussan, *Une histoire*, p. 56.

53. Y. H. Brenner, "Hu amar la" ("He told her"), in *Kol kitvei*, 6:29–33, cited in Anita Shapira, *Land and Power: The Zionist Resort to Force 1881–1948* (Oxford: Oxford University Press), p. 38. For a critique of Shapira, see Avi Shlaim, "The War of the Israeli Historians" (typescript of a talk at Georgetown University, December 1, 2003).

54. See Avi Shlaim, *The Iron Wall: Israel and the Arab World* (New York: Norton; London: Allen Lane, 2000).

55. *Dangerous Liaison*, transcript of interview with Benjamin Netanyahu, p. 11.

56. Shlaim, "The War of the Israeli Historians," p. 9.

57. Ibid., p. 6.

58. Jabotinsky, speech in Warsaw, July 12, 1938, cited in Bensoussan, *Une histoire*, p. 778.

59. Laor, "In Hebron," p. 33.

60. Ze'ev Jabotinsky, "Affen Pripatchok" (Samson's last words to his friends in the novel *Prelude to Delilah*), *Jewish Herald*, September 12, 1947, in *The Political and Social Philosophy of Ze'ev Jabotinsky*, ed. Mordechai Sarig, trans. Shimson Feder (London: Vallentine Mitchell, 1999), p. 30.

61. Netanyahu, *A Place among the Nations*, p. 366.

62. Ibid., p. 392.

63. Ibid., p. 371 (emphasis original).

64. Ibid., p. 370.

65. Ibid., pp. 360, 25; on Arab terrorism, see Netanyahu, *Fighting Terrorism: How the Democracies Can Defeat Domestic and International Terrorists* (London: Allison and Busby, 1996). The Jonathan Institute is named after Netanyahu's brother, who was killed in the raid on Entebbe. The proceedings of its second conference were published as *Terrorism: How the West Can Win*, which Netanyahu credits with having a major influence on Ronald Reagan and George Schultz and in persuading the United States to adopt a more preemptive policy against terrorism: "I believed that the key to the elimination of international terror was having the United States lead the battle, and that this American leadership would harness the countries of the free world into line, much as a powerful locomotive pulls the cars

of a train." He then argues that Israel was decisive in transforming the prevailing view of the 1970s and 1980s that "terrorism was the result of political and social oppression, [leading to] the inescapable conclusion that terror could not be eliminated without first bringing these conditions to an end. My colleagues and I rejected this view out of hand." In his contribution to the conference, Schultz credits institutions like the Jonathan Institute with influencing the policies of the "free world" on terror: "Can we as a country, can the community of free nations, stand in a purely defensive posture and absorb the blows dealt by terrorists?" This should lead us to revise or at least partly modify the view that Israel is simply hijacking Bush's "war on terror" in order to carry out its policies in the West Bank and Gaza with impunity, to the more disturbing view that Israel has partly determined those policies, playing an important role in persuading the United States to adopt its stance against terror long before 9/11. In his interview with me for *Dangerous Liaison*, Netanyahu commented: "Ronald Reagan read a book I wrote and according to Secretary of State Schultz, it influenced mightily the course of Reagan's thinking and therefore America's policy on terrorism, that is, towards a tougher policy." *Fighting Terrorism*, pp. 65–69; *Dangerous Liaison*, typescript of interview with Netanyahu, p. 6.

66. Netanyahu, *A Place among the Nations*, p. 365.

67. Ibid., p. 371.

68. Grossman, "Two Years of Intifada" (2002), in *Death as a Way of Life*, p. 177.

69. Ibid., p. 176.

70. Cited in Bensoussan, *Une histoire*, p. 836.

71. A. D. Gordon, "The Morning after the Debates on Voluntary Engagement" (1918), cited in Denis Charbit, *Sionismes: Textes fondamentaux* (Paris: Albin Michel-Menorah, 1998), pp. 577–78, in Bensoussan, *Une histoire*, p. 541.

72. Tom Segev, *One Palestine Complete: Jews and Arabs under the British Mandate* (London: Little, Brown, 2000), p. 452.

73. Pappe, *A History of Modern Palestine*, pp. 134–35.

74. Berl Katznelson to Mordechai Kushnir, Jerusalem, June 1918, in *Letters*, 2:529, cited in A. Shapira, *Berl. The Biography of a Social-*

ist Zionist: Berl Katznelson 1887–1944 (Cambridge: Cambridge University Press, 1984), p. 79.

75. Eliezer Steinmann, *Meoraot* (Tel Aviv, 1937), cited in ibid., p. 773.

76. Weizmann, *Trial and Error*, p. 30 (my emphasis).

77. Mirkin, cited in Marie Syrkin, *Nachmann Syrkin* (1900), cited in E. Luz, *Parallels Meet: Religion and Nationalism in the Early Zionist Movement 1882–1904*, trans. Lenn J. Schramm (Philadelphia: Jewish Publication Society, 1988), p. 341.

78. Moshe Leib Lilienblum, "The Way of Return" (1881), in Hertzberg, *The Zionist Idea*, p. 169 (my emphasis).

79. Cited in Bensoussan, *Une histoire*, pp. 642–43.

80. Cited in Yosef Gorny, *Zionism and the Arabs: 1882–1948* (Oxford: Oxford University Press, 1987), pp. 61–62.

81. Jabotinsky, "For the Sin We Have Committed," *Hayom*, March 3, 1940, in *The Political and Social Philosophy of Ze'ev Jabotinsky*, p. 40.

82. Jonathan Spyer, "Waking from the Oslo Dream," *Guardian*, May 1, 2003.

83. Shragai, "This Land Is Our Land," p. 11.

84. Grossman, "Arafat Arrives in Gaza" (1994), in *Death as a Way of Life*, pp. 8, 10.

85. Lilienblum, "The Resurrection of Israel on the Land of our Fathers" (1884), cited in Charbit, *Sionismes*, pp. 19, 21; in Bensoussan, *Une histoire*, p. 86.

86. Talmon, *Israel among the Nations*, pp. 9–10.

87. Sprinzak, "Three Models of Religious Violence," p. 480.

88. Buch is objecting to the nomination of refusenik David Zonsheine for the Nobel Peace Prize in 2004, *Ha'aretz*, October 8, 2004.

89. Ze'ev Smilansky, "From the Imaginary to Reality," *HaOlam* (1908), cited in Charbit, *Sionismes*, p. 366; in Bensoussan, *Une histoire*, p. 552.

90. Ze'ev Jabotinsky, "The Morality of the Iron Wall" (1923), cited in Charbit, *Sionismes*, p. 545; in Bensoussan, *Une histoire*, p. 457.

91. For a discussion of Zionism as based on a territorial concept of nationalism, see Oren Yiftachel, "Territory as the Kernel of the

Nation: Space, Time and Nationalism in Israel/Palestine," *Geopolitics* 7, 2 (Autumn 2002).

92. Emanuele Ottolenghi, "Anti-Zionism Is Anti-semitism," *Guardian*, November 20, 2003.

93. Avner Azulay, "Report of the Pan-European Jewish Roundtable" (Canisy, Normandy, January 30–February 2, 2004), p. 10.

94. Daniel Ben-Simon, Gideon Levy, ibid., pp. 3, 29.

95. Uri Avnery, "Manufacturing Anti-Semites," *Gush-Shalom*, September 28, 2002.

96. Yitzhak Frankenthal, "A Father's Plea to His Nation," *Guardian*, August 7, 2002.

97. Seminar of Communes, Gevat, September 10–October 10, 1943, cited in Shapira, *Land and Power*, p. 309.

98. Ben-Gurion, address to the Central Committee of the Histadrut, December 30 1947, cited in Masalha, *Expulsion of the Palestinians*, p. 176.

99. Cited in Masalha, *Expulsion of the Palestinians*, pp. 178–79. For a full discussion of Plan D, see Ilan Pappe, *The Making of the Arab-Israeli Conflict 1947–1951* (New York: Tauris, 2001), pp. 88–99, and *A History of Modern Palestine*, pp. 129–31.

100. Baruch Kimmerling, *Politicide: Ariel Sharon's War against the Palestinians* (London: Verso, 2003), p. 25.

101. Benny Morris, *The Birth of the Palestinian Refugee Problem Revisited* (1987) (Cambridge: Cambridge University Press, 2004). Morris's book has sparked off the fiercest disputes because he exposes the atrocities perpetrated against the Palestinians in 1948 while simultaneously arguing that the policy was justified. See Ari Shavat, "Survival of the Fittest," *Ha'aretz*, January 9, 2004, and responses, "The Judgement of History," *Ha'aretz*, January 16, 2004, and Morris's reply, "I Do Not Support Expulsion," *Ha'aretz*, January 23, 2004.

102. Sara Roy, "Save Your Outrage for the End," *Index on Censorship* 3 (2003): 206.

103. David Grossman, *See Under: Love*, trans. Betsy Rosenberg (New York: Simon and Schuster, 1989), p. 197.

104. Ibid., p. 380.

105. Ibid.

106. Ibid.

107. Ibid., p. 390.

108. Carl Sherer, letter to the *Guardian*, August 28, 2002.

109. Chacham, *Breaking Ranks*, p. 16.

110. Grossman, "The Holocaust Carrier Pigeon" (1995), in *Death as a Way of Life*, p. 13.

111. Ben-Gurion, *Memoirs*, 6:551 ff., cited in Segev, *One Palestine Complete*, p. 395.

112. Bernard Lazare to Theodor Herzl, February 4, 1899, cited in Nelly Wilson, *Bernard Lazare: Antisemitism and the Problem of Jewish Identity in Late Nineteenth-Century France* (Cambridge: Cambridge University Press, 1978), p. 245 (my emphasis).

113. Grossman, *See Under: Love*, p. 357.

114. Avnery, "Masada," *Gush-Shalom*, April 30, 2002.

115. "Hafkidi, Metzada, al homotayikh" ("Place Masada, Guardsmen, upon Your Walls"), *Ba-Ma'ale*, March 31, 1942, cited in Shapira, *Land and Power*, p. 315 (my emphasis).

116. Bensoussan, *Une histoire*, p. 787.

117. Grossman, *See Under: Love*, p. 25.

118. Lavie, "Hebron Diaries," p. 10.

119. Grossman, "The Holocaust Carrier Pigeon," p. 16.

120. "Report of the Pan-European Jewish Roundtable," p. 35.

121. Amir Ben-David, "In the Service of Refusal," *Ha'aretz*, October 1, 2004.

122. Grossman, *See Under: Love*, p. 67.

123. Roy, "Save Your Outrage for the End," pp. 208–9.

124. Avnery, "Revenge of a Child," *Gush-Shalom*, November 16, 2002.

125. Grossman, "Yes, Prime Minister" (1995), in *Death as a Way of Life*, p. 21; cited in letter from Joseph Eagle, "Apartheid Revisited," *Guardian*, July 24, 2002.

126. Lazare in Wilson, *Bernard Lazare*, p. 245. Compare Ahad Ha'am, in his critique of Herzl, "The Wrong Way": "[The point is] not to advocate this or that solution of the national problem, but to impart the knowledge which would enable the Jewish people to

understand itself and to decide which policy would be in line with its character and its potentialities," in Kohn, *Nationalism and the Jewish Ethic*, pp. 21–22. And Buber in 1949: "Nothing remains to us except the hope of reaching, via deep disappointments and difficult trials, via serious self-examination and the destruction of illusion . . . to a new juncture. . . . Today we cannot imagine it; we have no certainty of it, for from the point where we presently stand, it is much harder to get there than to any earlier point in the path." "Should the Ichud Accept the Decree of History?" p. 251.

127. *Confronting Views: Nine Photographers on the Israeli-Palestinian Conflict*, curated by Wim Melis (Groningen: Aurora Borealis, 2002).

128. Sara Roy, "The Revenge Must Stop" (unpublished, 2002), cited in Ellis, *Israel and Palestine Out of the Ashes*, p. 166.

129. Eliezer Steinmann, cited in Bensoussan, *Une histoire*, p. 773.

130. Micah Joseph Berdichevski, "In Two Directions" (1900–1903), in Hertzberg, *The Zionist Idea*, p. 295.

131. Weizmann, "The Ben-Gurion–Weizmann Controversy" (arguments delivered at private meeting, New York, June 27, 1942), in *Letters and Papers*, vol. 2, ser. B, pp. 492–93.

132. Bensoussan, *Une histoire*, p. 806.

133. Ronit Chacham, *Breaking Ranks*, "Introduction: Landmarks in the Israeli-Palestinian Conflict," p. 8.

134. Lavie, "Hebron Diaries," p. 10.

135. Chacham, *Breaking Ranks*, p. 27.

136. Ben-Gurion, *Israel*, p. 64 (emphasis original).

137. Ibid., p. 65 (my emphasis).

138. Ibid., p. 822 (my emphasis).

139. Ibid.

140. Hartman, *Israelis and the Jewish Tradition*, p. 17.

141. Cited in Shapira, *Land and Power*, p. 90.

142. Ben-Gurion, *Israel*, p. 792.

143. Ibid., p. 793.

144. Ibid.

145. Ibid., p. 794.

146. Ibid., p. 800.

147. Ibid., p. 802.

148. Ibid., p. 803.

149. Buber, "Should the Ichud Accept the Decree of History?" p. 251.

150. Scholem, "Encounter with Zion and the World (Decline)," in *The Fullness of Time*, pp. 87–89.

151. Azulay, "The Second Pan-European Jewish Roundtable," p. 10.

Index

Note: The first appearances of titles cited but not named in the text are listed by author with endnote and parenthetical text page.

Index